FICTION EDITING
A WRITER'S ROADMAP

FICTION EDITING

A WRITER'S ROADMAP

P.S. DOBIE

Lucid Editions
Vancouver

Published by Lucid Editions
4580 Main Street
Vancouver, BC, Canada
V5V 3R5

For permissions requests visit Lucid Editions—
www.lucideditions.ca

Cover design: Erek Tymchak

Fiction Editing: A Writer's Roadmap / P.S. Dobie. —1st ed.

ISBN 978-1-7752056-1-6

For AJ & Laurel,
avid readers

Contents

Preface

I had been editing fiction for a few years when it occurred to me that I was giving the same information to writers asking about my freelance editorial services. Most wanted to know:

- what's involved in an edit?
- how long will it take?
- what's the difference between levels of editing?
- how much does it cost?

I viewed answering the questions with each writer individually as a way to build trust and figure out whether we wanted to work together. And the answers did vary from manuscript to manuscript, depending on its word count and condition. But I also came to realize that the subtext ran deeper. What writers *really* wanted to know was:

- will editing make my book better?
- is it worth the money?
- why should I work with you?
- what if I don't like your advice?
- how do I know I can trust you?

As a fiction writer myself, I have been on both sides of the editorial exchange and I know that good editing can make a profound difference to your writing life. There are many excellent books on the craft of writing, but almost none for fiction writers who are trying to decide whether they need or want to work with an editor on their path to publication. Similarly, few books dissect the art and practice of fiction editing in any detail.

This book is designed to fill that gap.

Introduction

Writers who are thinking about working with a freelance editor are justifiably concerned about wasting time and money simply because they don't know what editors do and how they do it. Then there's the added problem of not knowing how to tell which editor is the right one for your work.

This book addresses those concerns. By the time you finish it, you'll know how to tell whether you need an editor and how to determine what level of editing you need. You'll be able to find the right editor for your project, and you'll know how to get the most bang for your buck. Finally, you'll see how good preparation and a solid understanding of the editor's role can lead to a rewarding experience and increase your chances of publishing success—not just for one manuscript but for all your writing.

Editors who seek craft advice can also use this book as a manual on how to approach all levels of fiction editing. It explains what skills and tools are needed and gives specific, step-by-step advice on how fiction editors work.

Part I of this book, **The Fiction Writer's World**, sets the context for those who write fiction today, looking at the two main paths to publication and examining why fiction writers work with freelance editors. What is it about the current publishing landscape that makes this a fairly frequent occurrence across all genres and publishing paths?

Part II, **The Editorial Landscape**, is a basic handbook on fiction editing. It will familiarize you with the levels of editing, describe what editors deliver, and walk you through the stages of an edit for fiction of all lengths. This section demystifies the process and lets you know what you can expect from a good edit.

Part III, **The Practical Writer**, is about how to prepare for an edit, how to DIY an edit if you can't afford an editor, how to tell a good editor from a bad one, and how to hone in on the right level of editing for your work. It also discusses how to approach revision once you have gotten your edited manuscript back.

In addition to these three main parts, a glossary defines terms used in the book and an appendix delves more deeply into what's involved in becoming a freelance fiction editor. A list of references and resources gives you further terrain to explore.

Please feel free to skip around inside the book. If you already know about the publishing industry, you might go straight to Part II. If you just want to find an editor and aren't that interested in how or why they do what they do, you might start with Part III. My hope is that the book helps you navigate the fiction writing world by providing essential information about an integral part of the journey to successful publication.

As all readers and writers know, the world needs more good stories. This book is designed to get your stories where they belong: in readers' hands.

PART I

THE FICTION WRITER'S WORLD

CHAPTER 1

The Writer's Goals

You've written a novel. It might be your first novel or your tenth, your first draft or your fourth. You might feel confident that it's the best it can be, or you might have doubts. You might have a plan for getting it published, or you might not.

First, congratulations on finishing your book. Wherever you are in your process, now is a good time to take stock of yourself, your manuscript, and your goals.

One way to understand what you want to get out of your fiction-writing life is to start at the end, with the people who will one day hold your book in their hands. Whether you self-publish or go through a traditional publisher, the final stop for your novel is the mysterious person known as "the reader."

People are still reading fiction. They're reading all the time. They're interested in stories. They're trying to find writers they will like. Some browse in bookstores or libraries; others work their way through prizewinners or best seller lists. Some use Goodreads; some rely on recommendations from Amazon. Many buy or borrow books that are recommended by friends or family. Escapism, literary fiction, gritty realism, romance, mystery—some readers love a particular genre or writer, while others read across genres.

You might not have a plan for reaching your readers while you're writing your book. You don't really need one when you're creating the first draft. But at some point, you will need to consider how you're going to get this particular novel to the people who will want to read it.

In an ideal world, your route to publication wouldn't matter. But the world has never been ideal for writers. Even in the novel's early days, the question of who might read it, and how they would access it, affected how it was written. Serialized novels like those by Charles Dickens or Wilkie Collins are an example of this dynamic in action. These novels were published in sequential installments, often in popular magazines. Many installments would end with a "hook"—a situation with an uncertain outcome or a burning narrative question—to ensure that readers would buy the next issue. Serialization allowed more people to read a writer's work since those who couldn't afford an entire book might buy a magazine. But it could also bloat the completed novel's word count due to the need for recapping and repetition, and many serialized novels were substantially reworked before they could be published as stand-alone books.

Whatever type of fiction you write, finding your readers requires knowing where booksellers will place your books on the spectrum of reading materials. Books are sorted into categories by online retailers, bookstores, and libraries in order to make it easier for readers to find books by browsing the categories they enjoy. Under the umbrella of commercial fiction, books are subsorted into genres such as mystery, romance, speculative fiction, historical fiction, horror, and many others. There are also age-based divisions, such as young adult or middle grade. Literary fiction, which is characterized by a very high standard of writing, might be shelved under its genre or found in the general or mainstream fiction section.

The Book Industry Study Group, an influential US trade association for the book industry, categorizes fiction according to Book Industry Standards and Communications (BISAC) codes, using standard alphanumeric descriptors for each category. For example, FIC065000 denotes Fiction / Epistolary, and FIC049040 denotes Fiction / African American / Historical. This idea of assigning a six-digit code to your work of genius might seem demoralizing, but as a fiction writer publishing in the twenty-first century, you should know about it. It's how things work. Category norms and genre expectations are a fact of the publishing world.

Readers expect certain things when they buy a novel. Mysteries must be solved. Romances must have happily ever afters. Historical and speculative fiction must create seamless and fascinating story worlds.

That doesn't mean that you can't write a unique and original novel. Good fiction transcends genre. No writer needs to adhere slavishly to the advice given in craft books or writing programs. There is always more than one way to tell a story and the right way is the way the writer chooses. After that decision is made, it's just a matter of pulling it off. This is where professional editorial feedback comes in.

....

Currently, the two main routes from writer to reader are traditional publishing and self-publishing. The latter is sometimes called "indie publishing," but since that term also refers to independent publishers (firms who publish books by more than one writer), in the interest of clarity I will use the term "self-publishing" to refer to the path taken by those who publish only their own work.

The following chapter takes a closer look at both main routes to publication—the ways, whys, and wherefores, as well as the pros and cons.

CHAPTER 2

The Publishing Landscape

Writing novels is not a get-rich-quick scheme and it's not a hobby: it's a way of life. Novels are mammoth projects. They take a certain amount of delusion, plus a certain amount of knowledge about what motivates you, plus a realistic assessment of your current skill level and how hard you're willing to work.

The same goes for publication. Choosing the right publication path for your current novel is not just about what's easy; it's about what works for your personality. As you read this book, consider your own assets, flaws, resources, and barriers in terms of time, money, patience, and willingness to learn. If you write full time and you're entrepreneurial by nature, you might want to publish your own work. If you write on the side and would rather not learn the business end of publishing, you will probably want to focus on finding a literary agent who will represent you or on submitting the manuscript directly to presses or imprints that publish fiction in your genre.

The membrane between traditional and self-publishing is getting more permeable all the time. A writer who's been published traditionally might move from a big publishing house to a smaller independent press or take over the publishing themselves, usually to get more support or have more control. Other writers, who have no interest in querying agents and publishers for months or years, will go straight into publishing their own work from the start. The good news is that once you've chosen a particular route for your current book, the dynamic state of publishing today means there is nothing to prevent you from crossing over from one type of publishing to the other down the road.

Traditional Publishing

If you're new to writing novels or to trying to get one published, the traditional publishing landscape can feel like a zoo. Most people involved in traditional publishing genuinely love books. But publishing is an industry, and books are its product. Producing books is expensive, and the publishing business, like all businesses, is focused on the bottom line. This makes complete sense from the industry's perspective. But from the writer's perspective, when you are querying agents and publishers, sending out your novel, and waiting for replies, traditional publishing can feel like a harsh and somewhat mysterious enterprise.

In the traditional publishing route, a publisher buys the rights to your manuscript and issues the book on your behalf. Traditional publishers in North America currently include the "Big Five" publishing houses as well as midsize and smaller independent presses. These publishing houses have editorial departments, where people known as acquisitions editors are responsible for finding and buying books that will sell.

The Big Five are entities formed by mergers of the major publishing houses of the twentieth century. They release thousands of books each year and have a large number of employees. Currently, they include Simon & Schuster, Macmillan, Penguin Random House, HarperCollins, and Hachette Book Group. Each of these large houses has several imprints, which operate more or less independently. Each imprint has its own "flavor," designed to appeal to a particular readership in terms of genre, subgenre, "feel," or other qualities of the books they publish.

Midsize presses include some university presses as well as established firms such as Sourcebooks or Graywolf Press. They typically publish anywhere from fifty to over a hundred titles a year. These publishers sometimes look at unagented manuscripts, although many don't. They can have many of the resources of Big Five imprints in terms of infrastructure and distribution, but advances and print runs might be smaller.

Small presses include regional publishers and digital publishers. They might publish anywhere from ten to over fifty titles a year; they have fewer employees and tighter budgets than the big publishers. Many small presses accept unagented manuscripts. They don't usually pay big advances, but they can give their writers more personal attention and might have a more collaborative approach.

Very small presses, sometimes called micro presses, might have only one or two employees. They might be longstanding firms with strong backlists, or they might be brand-new startups. They often run on shoestring budgets and are dependent on the owners' energy levels, business skills, and ability to find good manuscripts to stay afloat.

People in traditional publishing are under a great deal of pressure as they scramble to maintain revenues and profits. Fewer books are being bought in bookstores. Raising print book prices is getting harder to do, so publishers are trying to cut back the cost of production. Since the cost of paper and shipping isn't going down, this means cutting back on staff, which includes downsizing editorial departments. Trying to get more product out quickly puts more pressure on the remaining acquisitions editors, largely junior, to acquire books that don't need much work and can move quickly into production.

As a result, acquisitions editors often don't have time for deep editing. A copyeditor will work on the manuscript to bring it up to the house's quality standards, but novels that need a lot of work will rarely be bought.

At an editorial board meeting, an acquisitions editor must make a case for why the publisher should offer a writer a contract for a particular novel. The case involves not only the novel's quality but also its viability in the marketplace and its "fit" with the imprint. Because novels are such subjective reading experiences, and because publishing is such a pressure cooker of time and money, acquisitions editors must fall in love with manuscripts before bringing them to their editorial boards.

Publishers have rarely taken on a book strictly because of its merits. They consider what the reading public seems interested in, what sold well last year, what's being published in literary fiction magazines, and what's happening in movies, on television, and in the world at large.

Publishers pay attention to trends, but they can't really create them since trends begin with the spark that flies between creator and audience. In the world of books, the writer is the creator, the reader is the audience, and the traditional publishing industry is both the conduit and the barrier between the two. It's a conduit for books that are published, and a barrier for books that are rejected because they are unready or seem like too big a financial risk.

Where do literary agents fit in? Acquisitions editors often rely on literary agents as a reliable source of high-quality manuscripts they can fall in love with. Agents act as curators, bringing manuscripts to acquisitions editors they think will like that particular book.

If this way of finding novels that will sell sounds insane, maybe that's because it is. But it also works, at least from the publisher's perspective. The problem from the writer's perspective is that the system itself—the actual flow of money and product—has developed in such a way that the average fiction writer can feel like they're at the bottom of the dogpile when it comes to getting their work out into the world.

And there are plenty of writers these days. We have more free time, affordable technology, and writing programs than ever before. Agents and publishers receive an endless stream of manuscripts. Because there's such a high volume of product and such a small funnel for traditionally published books to enter readers' hands, it can be hard to get an agent, it can be hard to get your manuscript read by acquisitions editors at publishing houses, and it can be hard to get a publishing contract. Even if all that goes well, it's easy to have your book ignored. With two or three "seasons" in every year, publishers will put their promotional efforts into the biggest books on the new list for a few weeks, then move on to the next season's new books.

There are still good reasons to publish traditionally, perhaps the main one being that a professional publishing team will manage the editing, production, and distribution of your novel, which (at least in theory) will free up your time to write your next book.

How Traditional Publishing Works

First, you write the book. Then you make it as good as you can get it, either on your own or with help, paid or unpaid. Then you find out who's publishing that type of book. Depending on which publishing houses you're interested in, you might need to find a literary agent to represent you. This requires "querying"—sending agents a one-page letter and sometimes a few pages of the novel. If the agent likes your query, they'll read a page or two of the book. If you have kept their interest, they'll read more: ten or twenty pages. If they still like it, they'll ask for the rest of the manuscript.

If the novel lives up to its potential and they think they can sell it, the agent will contact you and offer representation. You'll have a phone call where they get a sense of what you'll be like to work with (and vice versa). If you accept their offer of representation, they will send the manuscript to specific acquisitions editors, ones they think will be interested in your book. The same process applies to unagented manuscripts but without the go-between—you send the query directly to publishing houses.

Eventually, if all goes well, you will get an offer of publication. From there, your book will be shepherded through the publication process. Some of the key steps in this process are copyediting, author review, final manuscript, design and layout, proofreading, final review, print and production, publication, and distribution. Related tasks will include cover design, obtaining recommendations for the cover, and writing catalog listings. The time frame from contract to publication can be eighteen months or so, depending on the publisher. If it's one of the season's top books for that publisher, you will have some help with publicity, marketing, and promotion.

Pros and Cons of Traditional Publishing

PROS:

- There is no cost to you except time, computer equipment, software, and Internet access.
- You will have access to a professional editing and publishing team at no charge.
- You will usually get an advance, although it might be small.
- You will spend less time managing the book's publication and distribution, which means more time to write.

- Your book will be made available in actual bookstores, libraries, and some schools.
- Your book will be more likely to get mainstream press reviews and will be eligible for more literary prizes.

CONS:

- It can take years, even decades, to get a first book published traditionally.
- In many cases, you will need to get an agent first.
- The publisher will contract for the rights to your work for a period, often five to ten years.
- Royalties are much lower than those for self-publishing.
- If you use an agent, they'll charge 15–20 percent (but not until they sell the book).
- You will have less creative control. Publishing is a collaborative process, and many professionals are involved in putting out a book.
- Marketing and publicity are still primarily in your hands.
- Publishers put their marketing efforts behind each season's new releases, which means that you have a limited time frame in which to drum up interest in your book.
- Bookstores don't keep big inventories, and the books that don't sell are returned and pulped.
- Your book might never earn out its advance, which means no royalties and perhaps a tougher sell for your next book.

Self-Publishing

If you are reading this book, you don't need me to tell you that self-publishing has exploded and is growing exponentially. Hundreds of thousands of novels are self-published every year in both digital and print formats, with audiobooks coming up fast. The *New York Times* includes self-published books on its best seller list. It's no longer called "vanity publishing," although the unwary writer can still be ripped off.

When you are the publisher, writing the novel is only the first step. Once it's written you become the quality control officer, production manager, promoter, marketer, and distributor. In order to find readers and sell copies, you're required to learn about search engine optimization, landing pages, Amazon algorithms, and ways to cultivate your readership and keep them engaged so they'll buy your next book. It's tougher to get self-published novels into bookstores and libraries, and keeping sales going means putting some of your time into marketing and distribution.

Self-publishing has various approaches. Hybrid publishers and book packagers will manage the process for you but cost more. Some of these take a percentage of sales and/or charge for services, or both. At the other extreme, a complete do-it-yourself experience has you subcontracting each nonwriting requirement individually.

In both traditional and self-publishing, the barrier between reader and book comes from the sheer quantity of books available through Amazon and other online retailers. There's a lot of product out there, and self-publishing writers need to learn how to find their readership and get the book into their hands without the help of a traditional publisher's systems and staff.

Self-publishing a book is like running a small business. It *is* running a small business. There is a learning curve, and the actual mechanics of self-publishing can be incredibly time-consuming.

How Self-Publishing Works

First, you write the book. Then you make it as good as you can get it, either on your own or with help, paid or unpaid. Then you either learn and DIY all the subtrades involved in publishing a book, or you contract them out. These include editing, cover design, interior design, and proofreading, as well as (for print) binding and printing. You can issue your novel by converting the Word file to an e-book before uploading it to a major e-book retailer, such as Amazon's Kindle Direct Publishing. You can also sell it on your own website, either as an e-book or a print version or both.

You might or might not set up a publishing entity and register for copyright. You get an ISBN (International Standard Book Number) for each format (hardcover, paperback, e-book, audio, etc.). If you quote from other published works, you check with their publishers for permission and possibly pay a fee. You write the sales blurb, jacket copy, or book description that tempts readers to buy. If you're making the book available in print format, you might use print-on-demand services to produce each book when it's ordered and paid for, thus avoiding the need to pay for up-front printing costs and storage space. Or you might work with a distributor and/or keep an inventory and distribute the print version yourself via your website or through back-of-room sales at readings and other events.

Regardless of how you print the book, you try to get the print version into those bookstores and libraries that stock self-published works. At the same time, you manage promotions, marketing, and publicity. This might mean arranging blog tours, podcasts, book readings, and press releases, along with any other strategies you can come up with to let readers know about your book. You do the accounting, manage vendor relationships, ask for reviews, and do all the problem-solving. In the meantime, you write your next book!

Pros and Cons of Self-Publishing

PROS:

- You have ultimate control and responsibility.
- Royalties are substantially higher than in traditional publishing.
- The timing of the book's release is under your control.
- You retain all rights to your work.
- The technology is getting easier to master every year.
- Once you find your readership and (ideally) get their contact information, it's easier to stay in touch with them and let them know when you have another book.

CONS:

- You have ultimate control and responsibility.
- No advance. In fact, you pay the up-front costs of manuscript preparation, publishing, production, and marketing.

- There will be a learning curve on the technical and promotional aspects of publishing, distributing, and marketing a book. This means you could be working evenings and weekends for weeks or months.
- It can be hard to get self-published novels into bookstores, libraries, and schools.
- Many in traditional publishing consider self-publishing less prestigious, and self-published books are ineligible for some literary prizes and reviews.

....

That's the publishing landscape in a nutshell. Like any industry, the more you learn about it, the stranger it seems at first. Then you internalize the situation and it normalizes. Think about competitive sports: the elite athletes know exactly what they're dealing with. By the time they get to the Olympics or the World Series or the Stanley Cup, they've seen it all. They are realistic about what it takes to get to play their game at that level, and they've figured out how they're going to take the steps they need to take to succeed.

The same is true for successful fiction writers. It's not necessarily the most talented whose books are on library, bookstore, and digital shelves. It's those who are still standing after everyone else has given up. Without exception, these writers have put time and energy into understanding themselves and their novel and figuring out how to get their book into the hands of their readers.

CHAPTER 3

Where Editors Come In

*My experience is that authors really depend on editors
for one thing: the truth.*

JAMES O'SHEA WADE

The purpose of all editing is to prepare a manuscript for publication. A strong manuscript is more likely to be well received by readers. Editing used to happen at the publishing houses. But with the concurrent rise of self-publishing and the downsizing of editorial departments in traditional publishing, as described in Chapter 2, it is now fairly common for individual writers to hire freelance editors. Some publishing houses also hire freelance editors to supplement their in-house editorial staff or to 'book doctor' a specialized project.

The biggest difference between freelance fiction editors and in-house acquisitions editors at publishers is that freelance editors don't acquire manuscripts for publication. They acquire clients, and they work on manuscripts, but they don't buy the rights to manuscripts or publish books.

You might think that only masochists would actually pay someone to tell them there's more work to be done on their novel. But it's more than masochism that motivates many writers—it's a hunger to improve and a willingness to do whatever it takes to get the best book possible.

Sometimes writers know their book's not quite where it needs to be, but they can't see the next step. So they call the manuscript "done," query and pitch agents, go to conferences, talk to publishers, or just go ahead and put the book out themselves, hoping for the best. Writers often rationalize their doubts about their manuscript with thoughts like, "there's no such thing as a perfect novel," or "maybe once I get a contract, the in-house editor will help me take it the rest of the way." As a writer, I've done this myself.

But most of the time, taking a difficult achievement like writing a novel all the way to the finish line needs some kind of mentorship. Athletes work with coaches, musicians work with teachers, business leaders work with consultants, and writers work with editors.

In practical terms, the main purpose of working with an editor before submitting or self-publishing a manuscript is to improve it in a more focused and effective manner than you could achieve on your own. Working with a good fiction editor can be viewed as a one-on-one writing workshop with your novel as the text. You learn more, you become a better writer faster, and you move the novel toward publication more quickly than you would by throwing the same flawed manuscript at the same hoop, hoping that one day it will go in.

Some writers work with an editor just to become a better writer. Getting one manuscript edited costs less than getting an MFA, and you can apply the lessons you learn from one manuscript to all your subsequent novels.

A good fiction editor will:

- identify your novel's strengths and weaknesses
- analyze issues that are interfering with the reader's experience
- provide specific solutions to fix the work at hand
- give you high-quality advice that will help you improve all your fiction, and
- motivate and energize you to engage in the hard work of revision.

A good editorial experience can also include helping the writer develop a realistic, knowledgeable outlook on the publication process. This means telling the truth about what it's like out there and being a reliable source of information and support.

Editors sound great, don't they? Maybe I'm biased, but I think many editors *are* great. They're helpful, they know many interesting things, and they can be a lot of fun at conferences.

Here's the question, though: is working with a freelance editor a necessary step in getting a novel published?

No.

There is no imperative to work with a freelance editor before you publish. Self-publishing writers do it if they are serious about quality control, and writers aiming for traditional publication do it if they are not getting anywhere with their manuscript, or if they want to get an objective assessment and specific advice to speed up revision.

Do You Need an Editor?

Deciding whether to look for a freelance editor can be difficult. You've got this novel, and you don't know if it's good enough to be published. You've read worse, but then again, it's hard to gauge your own work. The questions in the remainder of this chapter may help you decide whether working with an editor makes sense right now.

Has Anyone Else Read It?

You might know your manuscript inside and out, but what you can't see is the effect your work has on a reader: how it makes them feel. Maybe you've asked your friends or your family to read it. The problem is that most of your friends won't be able to tell you frankly if your book works. Similarly, your spouse can't tell you, your parents can't tell you, not even your writing group or workshop members can tell you. Everybody's seen what you put into it; everybody wants it to work.

So before you send the manuscript out or go ahead with self-publishing, try to find impartial readers (people you don't know) who are willing to read your manuscript for free and give you feedback. These people are often called beta readers. (For more about how to find them and what to ask for, see Part III.) It is important to test-drive your manuscript on regular people before you show it to professionals in the publishing world.

Have You Acted on the Feedback?

If you got feedback but stuck the notes in a drawer because they upset you, brace yourself for another look. Successful writers have thick skins when it comes to taking constructive criticism.

Take notes. If the feedback is from more than one person, look for common threads. First, pay attention to misunderstandings and lack of clarity. If your reader(s) misinterpreted characters or didn't understand plot developments, this is good information for you to have.

Second, be open to suggestions and ideas. You might experience an initial wave of rage and contempt for these buffoons who think they can criticize your work, but give it a few days and you might not only see their points but also generate a few ideas of your own about how to improve the book. You are under no obligation to change something just because a reader doesn't get it or doesn't like it. But if intelligent beta readers genuinely didn't understand something you thought was on the page, be glad that you got the opportunity to find that out before you went ahead with publication.

Are You Finished Revising?

If you can see things to fix in your manuscript, keep revising until you hit a dead end or can't take it anymore. Publishing an early draft or sending it to agents or publishers will burn bridges and cost you needless time and money. So will sending it to a freelance editor. Only once you've taken your best shot at revision and can no longer see what's needed, while recognizing that there's still work to be done, is it time to look for editorial feedback.

Has Your Writing Stalled?

After the previous point, it might seem contradictory to suggest that you can work with an editor on an unfinished manuscript or a very early draft. But sometimes that's the way to go. Maybe you know there's an issue with your work in progress, but you have no idea what it is. You are stymied and stop writing, unable to move forward. *If* you have written other novels and know that you have the stamina and wherewithal to finish a book-length work, then you might seek out a developmental editor or book doctor to get feedback on the story, or even on the outline, so you can identify the issue(s) and get back on track. The different types of editing are discussed in Part II, and ways to find your best editor are described in Part III.

Have You Queried Agents?

If you plan to publish traditionally, the least expensive way to see if your novel works is to query literary agents. Querying is also the most time-consuming and possibly the most frustrating way to test your manuscript's readiness. And, as mentioned above, you can burn bridges with potential agents if you query a novel before it meets traditional publishing standards.

If you have queried agents but haven't received any requests for a full manuscript, it could mean that you are querying the wrong agents or that there's a problem with your query letter. Or it might mean that there's a flaw in your novel's basic premise or that there are obvious issues around category norms or genre expectations. For example, if the word count is very low or very high, a novel can be hard to sell. First books are easier to get traditionally published if they are between 60,000 and 100,000 words (lower for children's lit). There are exceptions, of course, but they are often by authors with track records. Even J. K. Rowling started the Harry Potter series in the 75,000-word range.

If you have gotten a request for the full manuscript but haven't received an offer of representation, it could mean that the agent liked your query, premise, and the first few pages but doesn't think they can sell your novel to a publishing house. If you can't figure out why this is and they don't tell you, and if you would rather stick with this novel than start a new one, you may benefit from the clear, relatively objective feedback of a freelance editor.

Are You Unsure Whether It's Ready?

If you're planning to self-publish and are unsure about plunging ahead, think about the source of your uncertainty. If you have an intuition that the story could be better, listen to it. That intuition might not tell you what the problem is, but it can usually be relied upon as a sign that something is off.

Conversely, if you are sure your story works but you're not sure your manuscript is as error-free as humanly possible, consider getting sample edits from copyeditors (more on the types of editing can be found in Part II). If the samples reveal errors, you will probably want to have the entire manuscript copyedited. It is better to pay an editor to improve the manuscript to a publishable level than put it out prematurely and suffer through scathing reviews that will affect your sales.

....

This ends our discussion of you, the writer, and of your manuscript's place in the current publishing world. Now it's time to explore the landscape of fiction editing. If you do plan to work with an editor at some point, Part II will ready you for the journey and prepare you to make the most of your experience.

PART II

THE EDITORIAL LANDSCAPE

CHAPTER 4

Types of Editors

*Patience, the ability to take risks and to keep calm in
the midst of crisis, a real love of reading and a respect
for writers, and above all the gift of being able to see
what's wrong with a book (and what it might take to
fix it), together with a full reservoir of enthusiasm and
the kind of personality that can persuade a reluctant
writer who thinks his or her book is finished to
undertake one more rewrite—these are the qualities
an editor needs.*

MICHAEL KORDA

W ho are editors, anyway? There are editors for every subject under
the sun: business, math, science, the humanities, general
nonfiction, even poetry. Fiction editors work specifically with
novels, novellas, and short stories.

The fiction editor's main goal is ensuring that the reader becomes, and
stays, immersed in the story. At the line editing and copyediting stage, editors
show the writer exactly why and how a particular word choice or a badly
constructed sentence (or a string of them) might push the reader out of the
story. At the developmental editing level, editors alert the writer to the effect
on the reader of technical (craft) decisions related to bigger-picture elements

of the novel like flashback placement, POV shifts, the presence or absence of interior monologue, the dynamics of key scenes, the sequence of plot incidents, and so on.

A fiction editor is a (relatively) normal human being with a highly developed reading sensibility, editorial training, membership in one or more professional organizations, and often a higher-level education, such as a post-graduate degree in creative writing or English.

All fiction editors love stories. Mandatory personal qualities include strong insight and discernment, fierce analytical skills, and excellent writing and communication abilities. In addition, editors must understand the technical side of writing particularly well—the craft, if you will. This understanding allows editors to form a bridge between the reader and the writer.

Other than these common traits, editors are a diverse bunch. Many fiction editors write fiction themselves, both literary and commercial. Some teach writing. Some have worked in traditional publishing, while others have not. Those who haven't worked in publishing might have gained their experience at literary magazines, through degrees from university publishing programs, via certification from editorial associations, through mentorship on the job by experienced editors, or all of the above.

Some editors specialize in a certain level of editing (e.g., developmental only, or copyediting only), while others work at all levels. Some work in single genres, such as historical fiction, mystery, or speculative fiction, or certain categories, such as young adult or middle grade. Others work across genre and category. Some fiction editors also edit nonfiction, scripts, or other story-related materials, such as role-playing games.

Generally speaking, editors may be stronger in some aspects of editing than in others. A talented developmental editor can possess different and complementary skills to a meticulous copyeditor. Developmental editing requires the ability to see the big picture and to analyze what works and doesn't work. Being able to see a novel from a bird's-eye view is a skill not everyone has. On the other hand, some editors shine at scrupulous copyediting and have no real interest in taking apart a book at the macro level and seeing what makes it tick.

However, many editors have acquired strong skills at all levels of editing. Good freelance developmental and line editors with clients who self-publish will usually train themselves to be meticulous copyeditors as well, because their clients don't want to hunt around for someone else to do the final editing stages. They want someone they can trust to handle all levels of editing for their work.

The most crucial skill for any editor is an ability to articulate the experience of reading your book. Readers brings themselves to each book—in that way, reading is a collaborative act between writer and reader. Editors are basically professional readers who have the training and vocabulary to reflect on, analyze, and discuss your work. It's not just articulating the reading experience that's needed, but also an ability to sense what will improve it.

Developmental editors can hold your book in their mind's eye and see a shadow version of it simultaneously, a version where everything you've done well is still there while everything that detracts from the reading experience has been improved. Then they can join the dots between the two manuscripts—the actual and the possible—by describing what kinds of changes on the page can help you realize the most compelling version of your tale.

Line editors have a terrific "ear" for language and must be excellent writers themselves. They will suggest substitutions for overused words, cut away deadwood, ask questions, and generally get the writer thinking about creative solutions to issues. Sometimes a problem at the sentence level is a symptom of a bigger-picture problem. For example, the paragraph describing a character might be unclear, lack credibility, or contradict earlier information because, in fact, the character hasn't been developed enough to bear the weight of close scrutiny. In those cases, the most a line editor can do without veering into ghostwriting is point out the issue, suggest its roots, and offer some ideas regarding how the writer might get to the core of what's wrong.

Copyeditors know the fundamentals of language—grammar, spelling, usage—inside out, and they know when the rules can be broken. They are eagle-eyed, meticulous, and persistent in hunting down errors and finding the truth. They apply consistency and clarity to your manuscript, and they care about the details. They don't use Wikipedia (except for context) but go to the primary sources of truth. They've been known to reenact fight scenes to see why the action rings false, check the Bible to ensure the right verse is cited, and contact bureaucrats to verify a point of fact. Once a good copyeditor has taken your manuscript in hand, it becomes closer to the work of a professional writer.

....

A crucial skill for all types of editors is being able to communicate the issues with a manuscript honestly, without crushing the writer's soul. Most editors take it as a compliment to be called ruthless. At their best, they are also encouraging and kind.

It is the editor's responsibility to tell the truth about their experience as a reader—to let the writer know when their attention is drifting, character motivations are a mystery, dialogue is boring, setting is unclear, the plot is all over the place, the pacing is too slow, or the prose is confusing.

This doesn't mean you have to take every suggestion an editor makes. The editor's job, except for purely factual errors, is to make a case for how the reading experience can be improved by each suggested change. They must be clear and convincing, and this level of clarity and authoritativeness comes only from both understanding the craft issues and knowing the novel almost as well as you do.

That's the difference between the professional editor and your mom's friend who loves mysteries and thinks yours is as good as anything out there. Editors *know* what's out there. They know how to assess your novel's strengths and weaknesses and come up with concrete suggestions for bringing it to the next level. This is why many editors hold advanced writing degrees and/or write fiction themselves. They're as obsessed with writing as you are. They have to know their stuff. A good editor will never suggest tinkering unnecessarily with a novel that works. The first rule of any editorial interaction is "if it ain't broke, don't fix it."

CHAPTER 5

Levels of Editing

E ditorial definitions can be confusing, partly because no two editors will define a critique or evaluation or developmental edit exactly the same way, or even call them the same thing. For example, substantive editing is sometimes identified as content editing and sometimes as stylistic or line editing. The situation is complicated by the fact that there's overlap among types of editing. Improving plot and characterization (both big-picture aspects of the story) often means discussing scene dynamics. Improving scene dynamics often requires line editing to improve dialogue, action, or flow.

The Main Levels of Editing

Freelance fiction editors offer the following levels of editing:

- Big-picture (developmental or content) editing
- Substantive, stylistic, or line editing
- Copyediting

Big-Picture (Developmental or Content) Editing

This level of editing addresses holistic aspects of the novel such as structure, characterization, plot, point of view (POV), world building, pacing, braiding of characters and story threads, genre expectations, and other major elements.

Big-picture editing can be extremely helpful if plot is your nemesis or structure is a mystery. It can also help if your novel is far too long, or conversely, runs out of story only halfway through. It can help you find the protagonist's arc or throughline, locate and fix plot holes, diagnose pacing issues, and improve scene dynamics.

Depending on the thoroughness and timing of this edit, it might be called a developmental edit, a critique, or a manuscript evaluation. Its purpose is to discover what works, and what needs work, at the story level.

When considering a big-picture edit for fiction, think about how much detail you are looking for in the editorial feedback. This will relate to cost. Critiques and manuscript evaluations are "overview" editorial assessments. They will tell you if your story works and might also comment on its marketability and readiness for publication. They identify the story's main strengths and weaknesses and make suggestions on where to focus your revision efforts. They are typically less expensive than a full developmental edit because they are overviews and, therefore, less time-consuming to do.

Developmental edits are more thorough than critiques or evaluations. Also known as "book doctoring," developmental editing can happen at any stage in the writing process—on a complete manuscript, an early draft, or even on a partial manuscript or an outline. As well as an overview of what works and what needs work, a developmental edit will provide a thorough analysis of the novel and can suggest fairly specific fixes.

Depending on the manuscript's strengths and weaknesses, it will usually address not only holistic issues like characterization but might also comment on scene dynamics, dialogue, or prose issues (persistent writerly bad habits that detract from the reading experience). It could include a revision plan and might come with a book map, which is a grid or table that analyzes your novel's structure, plot, themes, and points of view. A book map can act as a helpful tool for making rewrites less confusing.

All big-picture edits (critiques, evaluations, and developmental edits) will include an editorial letter to the writer, summarizing the editor's feedback and offering suggestions for revision. This letter comes with the manuscript itself, which is often annotated with marginal comments so the writer can understand exactly how the editor experienced the novel, page by page or chapter by chapter. For more on these documents, see Chapter 6.

Substantive or Line Editing

In line editing, the editor pays serious attention to the prose itself. This involves a close, careful reading, examining sentences and paragraphs with the goal of improving clarity and flow, eliminating repetitions and redundancies, and pointing out unintentional contradictions or ambiguities. Sometimes called substantive editing, line editing might suggest reorganizing paragraphs, untangling sentences, tweaking chapter openings and closings, or even delving into scene dynamics, setting, and descriptions—for example, suggesting adding concrete details to bring a scene alive. Line editing is a talent and a skill born of long practice and requires that the editor be a good writer with a highly developed prose sensibility and an excellent ear. Good line editing will keep the writer's voice intact while raising the prose to its highest possible form.

When you start looking for an editor (covered in Part III of this book), review any sample line edits carefully to see if you are comfortable with the editor's skill level and their sensitivity to your manuscript's voice. It's a little like playing tennis—you want an editor who's at least as good a writer as you are, someone who can demonstrate on the page how to make your writing the best it can possibly be. But you don't want a powerhouse stylist who's going to override your own voice. It's always got to be your book, and any line editing should improve what's already on the page, identify deficiencies or problems with the prose, and push you to make every sentence count.

Copyediting

Copyediting is meticulous work at the level of sentences and words. It addresses spelling, punctuation, grammar, and word usage. Its goal is to remove mistakes and improve readability while preserving the writer's stylistic approach. It also checks continuity—for example, in character names and physical details, such as eye color. It sometimes includes fact-checking: place names, distances, titles, and so on. Some genres require more research than others. If your fiction relies heavily on correct knowledge of cars, guns, or military structure, you will want the copyeditor to either know about the topic or know how to research it.

A good copyedit can improve the reading experience simply by correcting errors that would otherwise affect the reader's ability to engage with the novel, such as dangling or misplaced modifiers, punctuation inconsistencies, and misused words. Readers might not be able to name the errors they're absorbing, but they will know something is wrong. Copyediting is the publisher's (or writer's) way of telling readers that they matter.

Copyediting is an important part of manuscript preparation. If you are looking for an agent or publisher, you don't need perfection, but you should try to remove errors. A sloppy manuscript won't be taken as seriously as a manuscript that's been prepared with attention to detail. Good copyediting can also improve your writing, and stronger writing is more likely to be read. If you are self-publishing, copyediting can save you from issuing a book with embarrassing and preventable mistakes.

Proofreading

Strictly speaking, proofreading is not editing: it's scrutinizing "proofs" or finalized page layouts for mistakes such as typos, missed edits, or formatting issues. Proofreading is a necessary step in the publication process, and it's done after all the other editing steps have been completed. It can't take the place of copyediting or line editing, simply because it doesn't correct sentence structure or flow. Only egregious errors will be flagged at the proofreading stage. Unlike other levels of editing, which are often done by the same person, proofreading is best done by someone who isn't already familiar with the book and therefore won't be blind to any remaining errors.

Editorial "Passes"

In cases where the manuscript needs a big-picture edit, a line edit, and a copyedit, the editorial process may be split into several rounds or "passes." A "pass" refers to one round of editing and is not synonymous with one read-through of the manuscript. A complex and detailed developmental edit might involve two or three read-throughs of the manuscript in one pass. During each pass, the editor has the manuscript in their possession for a certain period of time while that round of editing is carried out.

The first pass will usually look at the big picture. Because it might unearth issues that mean entire scenes could be removed or new ones written, there is little point in getting the manuscript line edited or copyedited simultaneously—why polish prose that could end up being cut? After the first pass, the writer will take the novel back and revise it. Some developmental editors will take more than one pass to work closely with the writer on developing the manuscript's elements bit by bit: characters, story arc, setting, and so on.

If the story changes radically during revision, some writers will get a second big-picture critique or a quick read-through to see whether the story works. More often, particularly for self-publishing writers, a second pass will consist of a line edit to focus on the prose itself at the level of paragraphs, sentences, and words, sometimes combined with or followed by a copyedit.

There might also be situations where a manuscript will receive multiple passes that don't involve developmental editing: one for line editing and another (or more than one) for copyediting, if the manuscript received a heavy line edit or has a large number of stylistic and mechanical errors. Most editors will work with what the writer—and the manuscript—needs.

In terms of scheduling, passes can take place weeks or months apart, depending on how quickly the between-pass revision goes. Some editors schedule the second pass in advance, while others ask the writer to contact them when the revision's almost done and schedule it at that point. Because revision times can be imprecise, the freelance editor can be a bit like an air traffic controller, scheduling manuscripts to land or sending them back up to circle around.

Whatever is agreed to will be reflected in the contract between writer and editor, which is worked out before the editorial process begins, and which can usually be changed with mutual agreement. For more on editorial contracts, see Part III.

CHAPTER 6

Editorial Tools

Getting editorial feedback can be a great experience but it can also be difficult for the writer to absorb unless it's presented with absolute clarity. This clarity should be the hallmark of the editor's deliverables, which can include some or all of the following items:

- An editorial letter
- The edited manuscript
- A book map
- A style sheet
- Meeting(s) and correspondence between editor and writer

The Editorial Letter

Novels are complicated, and writing is an art, a craft, and a skill. Recommendations for revision can be wide-ranging and complex. But writers don't have an endless capacity for absorbing feedback on their book. It can be overwhelming to have minor tweaks mixed into a list with larger suggestions and dumped unceremoniously into your lap. Therefore, it's the editor's job to organize the feedback so that the writer can make sense of it. The main tool at the developmental level is the editorial letter.

The editorial letter contains observations and recommendations, categorized and prioritized to make it easier for the writer to absorb the information. These letters can range in length from three to thirty-plus pages, depending on the editorial scope of work, the level of detail, and the number of suggestions offered.

Although for the reader, big-picture aspects of a novel are not experienced separately, editorial letters by necessity discuss them separately. This might mean grouping related problems, such as issues with both dialogue and scene dynamics, under an umbrella category, such as characterization or plot.

A good editorial letter will discuss both what works and what needs work. *What works* (a.k.a. "strengths") must be discussed because writers might not know they're succeeding with certain things, and there's a very real risk that they'll revise the good stuff out of the manuscript along with its problems. *What needs work* (a.k.a. "weaknesses") discusses the issues that interfere with the reading experience. This section usually receives much more page time in the letter than what works, but it's important to discuss both.

It's part of the editor's job to make suggestions clear and more or less manageable, presenting them as a springboard to revision. In addition to suggestions about the specific manuscript, some editors include, as part of their letter, teaching notes on persistent writing problems. For example, if characterization or point of view is an issue, I might give tips on how to reveal character more clearly, how to adjust psychic distance, how to write better dialogue, or how to analyze a scene's dynamics and find the core conflict to make it more compelling. If the novel has an episodic feel or momentum stalls, I will usually include tips on how to look at the story's cause-and-effect chain and make sure that scenes build on each other. Nonlinear stories can work beautifully, but if I have a nonlinear story that doesn't work, there is usually a way to address the problem without reorganizing the story's structure. It's not about changing the writer's approach, but rather about pointing out issues and suggesting solutions. I might also suggest a specific book about the craft of writing or point the writer to excerpts from published novels that demonstrate on the page how to do a particular thing really well.

A note about craft books: they can be useful, but they can also be overly prescriptive. By their very nature they give general rules or imaginary constructs—things like where turning points should take place or how structure should work. They can be helpful in articulating particular strategies and in illuminating things to try in a revision, but they can also be overwhelming and counterproductive when you're actually trying to write or revise the book. They can't take into account your specific novel's "soul."

If the edit is being done in two or more separate passes—first a big-picture critique or developmental edit, followed (after revision) by a line edit and/or a copyedit—there will be an editorial letter for each pass. In a two-pass edit, the second editorial letter is usually shorter. It will discuss the revision, comment on anything that still needs work, and list the main copyediting decisions.

The Edited Manuscript

The manuscript is the next deliverable. The editor will return it to the writer, saved with a new filename. This edited manuscript forms the basis of the writer's next draft. Most editors work on manuscripts electronically, using Microsoft Word because of its large market share and the number of publishing employers that insist on it. When editing electronically, editors use Word's features: marginal comments and Track Changes.

Every editor has their own style in marking up a manuscript, and most will tailor the amount of markup to the level of edit they're doing. For example, during a first, focused read-through for a developmental edit of an 80,000-word novel, I might insert several hundred marginal comments with my thoughts on character, scene dynamics, plot issues (large and small), setting, world building, and prose. These comments give the writer my detailed readerly reaction to their story as it progresses, scene by scene. Comments might also touch on structure and suggest combining or splitting chapters, point out inconsistencies, and raise questions. For a critique or evaluation on the same manuscript, I might comment only half as much.

I insert marginal comments as I'm reading, in a stream-of-consciousness way, without censoring. Later, I might go back and delete comments that are irrelevant or annoying, but on the whole, I think it's interesting for a writer to see what a reader's thinking—to "read over my shoulder," as it were.

Editors vary on the level of detail they'll put in a comment. One editor might ask, "What's X's motivation for checking the cellar? The reader needs to know," while another editor might say, "Consider having Y tell X about the missing photo album, to motivate X's entering the cellar."

Marginal comments for a line edit are usually smaller in scope, querying word choice, pointing out discrepancies, or giving the rationale for moving or cutting text. In a copyedit, comments are fewer, limited usually to necessary queries or explanations. Comments take time, so editors on a tight deadline or with a limited scope of work will use them sparingly.

The feature Track Changes allows the editor to mark up the text with redlines—proposed corrections or improvements—right on the screen. In line editing, I might suggest moving blocks of text or ending chapters on a different sentence or word in addition to offering other feedback. In copyediting, punctuation and spelling are corrected right on the page. The writer will get back the edited manuscript covered with Track Changes and then accepts or rejects each suggested edit during the revision process. See the back of this book for a link to examples of edited manuscript pages.

The Book Map

The term 'book map' has more than one meaning—some people use it to describe a book's outline, especially for nonfiction, while others are referring to a one-page mind map that helps you generate ideas for your book.

In my world, a book map for fiction is basically a scene list, usually in a spreadsheet or table format, that charts the novel's chapters and scenes in order. The chapter and scene numbers run in rows down the book map's left-hand side, and columns run across the top. Column headings in the book map vary and might include chapter number, word count, location, date, what happens, POV, notes on character arc, turning points, special objects, or other information that the editor pulls out for analysis. A short novel might have a two-page book map, while a long, multi-POV novel might need fifteen legal-sized pages.

Some writers use book maps to help them keep track of what's going on in the novel. Authors like Joseph Heller, J. K. Rowling, and Jonathan Evison take various approaches to mapping out their works in progress. See the back of this book for a link to examples of book maps.

The Style Sheet

At the copyediting stage, an editor will often create a "style sheet" specific to the novel or series of novels. Here they will document the choices made in terms of punctuation, capitalization, style, and unusual spellings so that when the writer goes to revise, they have a clear record of these minor but important editorial decisions. The style sheet might also list character and place names, continuity notes, and other information that will help the writer preserve consistency. Style sheets are a useful tool not just for the writer and copyeditor, but also for the proofreader.

The style sheet is created with guidance from two main resource documents: a dictionary and a style guide. In North America, the standard guide for fiction is *The Chicago Manual of Style: The Essential Guide for Writers, Editors, and Publishers,* a gigantic book first published in 1906 and updated regularly since. It sets out whether to show numbers spelled out or as numerals (one or 1), whether to capitalize words like "sir," how to abbreviate, how to show foreign terms, how to use punctuation correctly, and so on. UK fiction editors use different style guides, such as *New Hart's Rules: The Oxford Style Guide* or *Butcher's Copy-Editing.* Newspapers and magazines that publish fiction use their own house style guides.

Most editors will use a preferred dictionary, such as *Merriam-Webster's Collegiate Dictionary* or (in the UK) the *Oxford English Dictionary,* either in print or online or both, to verify spelling, hyphenation, capitalization, and so forth. Depending on the story world (military fiction, for example), an editor might also use more specialized reference materials.

The objective of the style sheet is to keep track of details, thereby improving consistency with more efficiency. See the back of this book for a link to examples of style sheets.

Writer and Editor Conversations

After getting back the manuscript, editorial letter, and other associated documents, most writers need a few days or weeks to absorb the information. Sometimes it's demoralizing to see how much work an editor is suggesting. Sometimes questions arise or a suggested revision needs more discussion. At this point, a meeting (in person or remote) between writer and editor can put everything into a new perspective. As a writer, you will never regret the chance to talk to someone who knows your book almost as well as you do.

Freelance editors usually schedule calls in advance. During the call, editor and writer will discuss the book, explain, ask questions, talk about motivations or plot issues, and work out revision strategies. Some editors include this call in the cost of an edit, while others charge an hourly rate.

The writer/editor conversation won't just be a rehash of the editorial letter and the comments. It will be a living thing, and it might even be fun. At the very least, it will reassure the writer that editorial suggestions don't come with a big stick. For example, the writer might bring up one of the issues raised in the editorial letter and explain why the suggested fix won't work for them, or what they fear they will lose by taking it. Then the editor can ask questions, suggest a new angle, or even just express sympathy and support. Together they can noodle around additional possibilities and give the writer more juice for revision.

....

The editorial letter, the manuscript itself, the book map, and the style sheet are the main tools fiction editors use to deliver their services to writers. Each addresses a specific need, and each reflects your novel in all its uniqueness. The next chapter explains how editors actually do the work.

CHAPTER 7

What Developmental Editors Do

*If the short-term goal of developmental editing is the
best current book, the long-term goal is the maximum
development of the writer's talent and independence.*

PAUL D. MCCARTHY

W riters are an individualistic bunch. Whether you're a planner (outliner) or a pantser (writing "by the seat of your pants"), there are as many ways of writing a novel as there are people.

Editing is also an individual pursuit, but there is a natural flow of events that most fiction editors will follow, to one degree or another. So it is possible to describe a "standard approach" involving sequential steps—depending, of course, on the contract's scope of work and the editor's personal style.

Developmental editing is sometimes called book doctoring or content editing. As described in Chapter 5, it can range in detail from a full developmental edit to an overview critique or a manuscript evaluation.

This chapter describes two approaches to developmental editing. The first details my typical approach to a developmental edit of a completed novel. The second describes how editors do ongoing story development, coaching, or consulting with writers.

If you're working with an editor at a publishing house, its in-house editors are unlikely to have time to give your manuscript the level of scrutiny described below. Then again, the very fact that your novel has been acquired for publication probably means there's not much work to be done. For reasons discussed in Chapter 2, in-house editors rarely acquire manuscripts that need substantial work.

How Developmental Editing of a Complete Manuscript Works

I use the following approach for big-picture (developmental or content) editing. This involves five stages:
1. Understanding the novel *as it is*
2. Diagnosing issues
3. Considering context
4. Identifying solutions
5. Telling the writer

Stage 1: Understanding the Novel As It Is

In a big-picture edit, my first step is to read the manuscript from beginning to end. If I'm doing a manuscript evaluation, this might be done at an almost-normal reading speed (or a bit slower than normal). If I'm doing a more detailed and intensive developmental edit, it will be a close reading. A close reading is not how most people read a book. It's a very concentrated, focused reading that absorbs and analyzes the story sentence by sentence, paragraph by paragraph, page by page, scene by scene, chapter by chapter.

Whether I'm reading closely or at a more normal speed, I mark up the manuscript with marginal comments as I go through the story. Leaving a trail of my thoughts about the initial reading experience helps me to analyze a novel's strengths and flaws.

During this first reading I will enter the story world, meet the characters, immerse myself in the reading experience, and observe how the story is told—its structure, plot threads, character arcs, and other integral elements. By the time this first reading is done, I will have a good understanding of the novel and will have identified any obvious issues interfering with the reading experience. Where did I drift, where did I stop believing, where did I see plot holes? Just as important—in fact, more important—is my developing sense of what works and why it works. What do I love about this story, these characters, the time and place of the story world? If I found it in a bookstore, would I take it to the cashier?

Then I will read the novel a second time, usually more quickly, and do a structural analysis. I will, at this point, often create a book map. A manuscript isn't just an experience, it's also a physical object (whether it's electronic or in print), and it can actually be taken apart and analyzed. I use the book map as a diagnostic tool, usually for issues with structure or pacing. It's a bit like reverse engineering. It allows me to look at word counts, see when POV shifts, note placement and length of flashbacks, trace character development, look at which incidents are dramatized in scene and which happen "off stage," if you will, and try to confirm or refute my initial impressions about what's stopping the reader from fully engaging with the work.

Stage 2: Diagnosing Issues

How can an editor tell what a novel's issues are?

It's true that reading is a subjective experience. However, a story's flaws can be identified and described in surprising exactitude by professional readers, just as an athlete's performance can be assessed and its weaknesses analyzed by professional coaches.

Big-picture issues in fiction can be found in the following areas:
- What it's about, what happens, and how it unfolds (the premise, storyline and plot)
- Who it's about (characters)
- How the story is told (POV, psychic distance, narrative strategies)
- The work's lucidity and coherence
- The quality / style of the writing, and
- The setting and management of the reader's expectations

Each of these areas can be broken down into much more detail, of course. Here, not necessarily in order, are the things I consider.

CHARACTERIZATION

I look at who the characters are, what they want (or don't want), whether they get it (or try to prevent it), and how they change over the course of the novel. If two characters are fulfilling the same purpose, can they be conflated to better effect? If motivation is helped by creating a stronger connection between two characters, can their backstories be linked, or could a present-time scene be changed or added? I almost never propose adding a new character but might suggest changing who does what, for example, to take advantage of who has access to information or to otherwise improve the plot.

PLOT

I analyze how the story is told—what happens, in what order, from whose point of view. What is happening that makes it worth telling a story, and have those events been ordered into a compelling reading experience? In examining plot, I explore whether any scenes might be missing or whether too many scenes do the same thing. I look at whether plot developments could start earlier, end sooner, or be improved by better braiding of subplots and story threads. I form an opinion on whether there is fat that can be cut or developments that can be realized more fully.

STRUCTURE, NARRATIVE DESIGN AND FLOW

Readers won't necessarily notice a novel's structure. They will know only whether they want to keep turning pages. Craft books might say there has to be rising action and a denouement that involves X, Y, and Z, but each story has its own soul. The story's true shape is revealed by everything in it, and the writer decides what to put in and what to leave out.

Three-act structure has a beginning, middle, and end, but it's not the only way to tell a story. The novel's structure might be traditional or nonlinear or a combination or something new entirely. The question is, does it work?

If something about how the story is designed stops me from wanting to turn the page, then I look carefully to see what's happening. I examine the story's overall arc and see whether scenes can be moved, cut, or rearranged to achieve greater drama or a more compelling flow. I use the book map to break down word counts, see where scenes take place in the overall structure, and assess how these scenes develop character arcs. If the story feels episodic or fails to gather momentum, I will map out the novel's cause-and-effect chain and its timeline. A long flashback that starts on page two can be an obvious issue, but there are subtler ones as well, to do with modulation of tension. Sometimes moving a scene makes all the difference, even if you don't change its content or alter the scenes around it, because juxtaposition can create its own surprises within the text.

POINT OF VIEW (POV)

I also examine point of view and psychic distance. Does the narrative approach—first person or third, close or objective, past tense or present—create a barrier to reader engagement with the character(s)? This is particularly crucial for a novel's opening chapters, where the reader is still deciding whether to engage with the story. Readers are ruthless with their time and attention. If they can't get into a book, they will put it down and walk away.

POV is not cut and dried—rather, it flows in and out. Third person can range from being entirely inside one character's perspective to full omniscience. It's related to psychic distance—are we inside the character's head, an arm's length away, a block away, or on the moon?

Overall, the question is whether the POV approach works for this particular book. It's rare that the writer's POV choice will feel completely at odds with the book's content. But sometimes POV is handled clunkily and draws attention to itself, and sometimes the wrong psychic distance creates a missed opportunity for deepening a scene's emotional impact. As a writer, I have revised my own novels from third person to first person (and vice versa) and have experienced firsthand how changing POV can have a profound effect on the reading experience.

THEME

I hesitate to use the word theme when discussing novels, simply because so many fiction writers don't write with a theme in mind and find it difficult or galling to apply the concept to their work after the fact. As a fiction writer myself, I used to think themes were something that academics resorted to when reviewing someone else's creative work, trying to figure out the writer's position on a topic by picking apart their novel. Needless to say, if the writer had a particular position and could express it in a sentence, why go to the trouble of writing an entire novel?

However, my thinking around theme evolved after I got a novel of my own edited and the editor asked me to try coming up with a thematic statement. After some struggle and resistance I did it—and lo, a ray of light came down from the heavens and illuminated the problems with my story. It let me rewrite the ending and reorder plot events. It showed me that I must cut one quarter of the scenes and write new ones. It even saved one of my characters from death.

So now, if I am editing a manuscript and find myself having trouble understanding character motivations, or if important goals and desires seem to flip flop in an incomprehensible way, or if the story fails to build, or the characters don't grow, I will raise the topic of theme in the editorial letter as a way of encouraging the writer toward developing a lens through which to focus the material.

For me, the most illuminating way of exploring theme is to consider whether there's any central idea that the novel is expressing and whether you can develop a question or statement about it that sheds light for you, the writer, on what to do with characters or the problems they encounter. Maybe the question has to do with (say) the cost of choosing private obsessions over family connections. Sometimes applying this question or statement to each person in the story, especially those who don't feel integral to the work's fabric, will tell you a lot about how characters can develop, and even about which characters should stay and which ones might go.

Thematic elements can also be seen at the paragraph level. Sometimes the writer might not be aware of a repeated underlying metaphor or thread that, with a bit of adjustment, could give the work an added sense of coherence and lucidity that enriches the reading experience. It's not a matter of shoe-horning images of birds or water or another leitmotif into every scene. You don't want readers feeling like every page is designed to hit them over the head with a particular message or meaning. However, during a developmental edit I will notice thematic elements, see how they magnify or intensify the reader's emotional experience, and consider whether they might be strengthened or supported with a bit of tweaking.

It's never too late to think about your novel's thematic underpinnings. On the other hand, sometimes there's no need to spend editorial time analyzing theme. If the novel works, it works. You don't need to explain anything with your story. The reader's compulsion to turn the page comes from more than one desire—they want to see what happens, they want to understand something new, they want to have an experience, and probably most importantly, they want to spend time with your characters and keep feeling the way they feel as they read your work.

PROSE

I consider the quality of the writing itself, paying particular attention to clarity, style, and voice. Even if line editing is not included in my scope of work, if the prose is weak I will sometimes make a list of writerly tics that detract from the reading experience. Depending on the writer's experience level, I might pull out essays, articles, and examples to send along with the edit itself. Sometimes I just mark up persistent issues in the manuscript and offer suggestions for improving prose, like strengthening verbs, reducing an overreliance on adverbs, or being more ruthless with wordiness. I will sometimes line edit a few paragraphs or a whole scene to illustrate what I mean.

READER EXPECTATIONS

Publishing categories and genre norms influence a reader's expectations of a book. Each novel also tells the reader what to expect from its very first sentence or paragraph. These early sentences might be seen as the novel in miniature, in a way; they teach the reader how to read it. So if you start a novel with exquisite prose and (say) a leisurely description of character or setting, the reader is prepared for one type of reading experience, whereas if you open *in media res* with high action and a gritty tone, the reader's prepared for a different experience. Each novel will, of course, move between intensity and quietude, and writers have tons of latitude in how they take the reader through the story. But sometimes manuscripts begin one way then switch to a different writing style entirely, which can fragment the reading experience and leave the sense that it lacks cohesion and unity. If that's the case I would identify where the voice or approach changed, and potentially suggest going back to the original impetus for the story as a way to help the writer clarify what it's really about and what they are giving the reader.

....

While I'm doing all this big-picture thinking I make notes, either on lined paper, in the book map, in the manuscript itself, or all three. Then I go back to the manuscript and read over my marginal comments. Sometimes I read the novel a third time if it's very complicated or if the issue is very subtle.

And yes, occasionally there are no major issues, in which case I congratulate the writer and spend the editorial letter telling them what I liked and how their novel made me feel as a reader. I don't suggest changes unless I believe they will improve the book, and it's always the writer's decision whether to try them out.

Once I have a good idea of the manuscript's main strengths and weaknesses, I start working on the editorial letter. Using a Microsoft Word add-in software called PerfectIt, I extract all my marginal comments into a separate document. Depending on the depth and detail of the edit (which relates to the turnaround time and fee), I either just skim through the comments and then write the editorial letter, or I sort comments into categories such as characterization, pacing, and structure as preparation for writing a detailed analysis and coming up with specific revision advice.

At this point, I try to take a short break from the manuscript, at least a couple of nights, and let my subconscious do its work while I go about other business. Then I'll return to the manuscript with fresh eyes, able to dive deeper, prioritize, and articulate the issues I have encountered.

Stage 3: Considering Context

This is when I take my eyes off the manuscript and consider category norms and genre expectations, which, as mentioned earlier, are a fact of the publishing world. We want thrillers to be gripping and mysteries to keep us guessing. I try to place the novel on a metaphorical bookstore's shelves. An unusually high or low word count might make it tough to sell to traditional publishers. Timing is a factor, too—in genres like historical fiction, time periods can go in and out of fashion. If the novel's set in a time period that's been oversaturated or features character types who have been overused, it might need a fresh approach or a "twist." This is especially true for novels being submitted to traditional publishers. It can be chilling to see how quickly acquisitions editors dismiss manuscripts that are riding a dying trend.

Stage 4: Identifying Possible Solutions

In this stage of the edit, I go back to my thoughts on the novel itself and begin to organize them in order of importance. If I'm doing a critique or a manuscript evaluation, I might identify the biggest issues and suggest general remedies, leaving the writer to figure out the details. If I'm doing a developmental edit, I usually have a longer list of issues, a more specific analysis, and suggest possible remedies in much more detail. Not just "make Harry more sympathetic," but "on page nine, consider having Harry do this." Not just "improve Angela's motivation for getting involved with the cult," but "in scene two, consider having Angela form an emotional connection with the little girl who later goes missing by discovering a shared interest in animals."

The main editorial task here is to be creative and empathetic while recognizing that it is entirely up to the writer whether they think a suggestion works or doesn't work. I have an opinion, and it's my job to convey it and support it with explanations and examples. But it's always the writer's book.

If a suggestion is complicated, I try to bolster the writer for the enormity of the task. In fiction, it's rarely a matter of removing a chapter. Issues can be complex and so are the solutions. If two characters would be better as one, little bits and pieces must be rewritten all the way through the novel and scenes might be dropped or drastically conflated. If the plot is too convoluted or lacks propulsion, it might mean adding or cutting a storyline or improving the novel's cause-and-effect chain to build more cohesively toward the climax. If point of view is an issue, it might mean rewriting entire scenes or learning how to transition more smoothly from one POV to another by passing what writer Richard Russo calls "the narrative baton." Or if all the scenes have the same tempo, it might mean slowing important moments down with concrete sensory details, interior monologue, or other slow-motion writing techniques.

At a more global stylistic level, remedies might include suggesting that the writer rework the dialogue in key scenes, improve scene dynamics, or make adjustments to the balance between events that happen "in scene" and those relayed by narrative summary or exposition. I might suggest alternate word choices (stronger verbs or more precise nouns), remove repetitions or awkward phrasing, or move text for better clarity or flow. Here we veer into line editing, and that's all right. Editing is an art and a craft, and there will always be overlap between the levels.

Truly unfixable issues with a manuscript, ones that require starting over from scratch, are rare. They usually come from a writer's inexperience and might stem from basic problems such as not having the required level of skill as a writer or not having enough "story" or a strong enough premise to sustain a book-length work. By the time a novel reaches a professional editor, the issues might seem too complex or big, or too challenging or hopeless, but a good editor will discuss the problems and their potential remedies in a way that shows the writer how to approach the rewrite while supporting and encouraging the writer's vision for the book.

Stage 5: Telling the Writer

This part requires both tact and deep honesty. Issues and recommendations must be communicated in a way that gives the writer the wherewithal to proceed. The editor must frame the work to be done in such a way that the writer will not only understand the manuscript's strengths and weaknesses but will want to put in the work needed to address its flaws and distortions, always with the goal of bringing it to a higher level.

The editorial letter is the primary delivery vehicle for editorial feedback, particularly for big-picture edits. The edited manuscript itself runs a close second. I send the editorial letter, manuscript, and book map (if there is one) by email as Word attachments. At this point, I will also ask the writer to take their time reviewing the material and then get back in touch to let me know what they think.

Ideally, we will talk about the book within a week or two of the writer receiving the edit, either before they start their revision or as they work their way through it.

How Editorial Coaching Works

Editorial coaching can work well for writers who are struggling with story development for a novel or series, who want a one-on-one learning experience, or who work best with external deadlines to help them produce.

Coaching can include any or all of the following interactions:

- Written feedback on an outline or a partial manuscript
- Video conferences to talk through the story, identify connections, develop characters, generate ideas, and motivate the writer to keep going
- Developmental feedback, and sometimes substantive editing, on chunks of a manuscript, providing guidance to the writer as they work their way through the novel. This feedback includes direct commentary and line editing on the manuscript chunks, and resources (craft essays or excerpts of published fiction) that I think will help with the particular writerly problems the chunk displays. It also includes email correspondence and video conferences to discuss the book. This approach is similar to the "packet" exchange model used in low-residency MFA programs, except that the exchange is between writer and editor rather than student and teacher.

My usual process for this type of developmental editing is to first understand the writer's specific goals and impediments, then talk about how I can help move them forward on the project at hand. At heart, it's a teaching relationship that uses the writer's current project as its textbook. For writers working on a novel series it can be particularly helpful in getting the overall big arcs down and identifying the best spots to begin and end each book within the series.

Because each writer and each novel is different, the initial interaction usually involves gathering information and talking about the writer's challenges. From there I will suggest a scope of work and rough schedule, including milestones. We'll use these to arrive at a mutually agreed-on plan that has room to change with the writer's needs.

Because this type of consulting is billed at an hourly rate it's less of a one-shot financial commitment than the developmental edit (or critique or evaluation) of a full manuscript. It can address specific issues as they arise and provide targeted exercises and feedback on specific weaknesses, in a way that one-time editing of a novel usually doesn't. It can also be stopped at any time and restarted when the writer's time, funds and energy permit.

Writers react differently to editorial advice. It can feel like an intimidating process initially if you are unprepared, but working with an editor shouldn't make you want to stop working on the novel. If it does, you are with the wrong editor. I have a careful approach to accepting manuscripts for editing because I want to work with writers who are prepared to push themselves. They don't always take my advice, of course, but that's really not the point. The point is to give the writer a new way of looking at the novel and the tools to get it into the best possible shape.

CHAPTER 8

What Line Editors Do

The line editor is supposed to be a book's ideal
reader, the one who asks all the questions and heads
off all the problems in a book so that it is satisfying—
rather than maddening, confusing, or just a little too
dull to finish—to other readers.

GEORGE WITTE

A novel that is structurally sound, with strong characters and a compelling story, can still be painful to read if the prose is weak, scenes are clunky, or sentences are bloated, badly constructed, or peppered with clichés. In such cases the reading experience is destroyed bit by bit in a death by a thousand cuts.

As literary fiction sometimes demonstrates, great writing can draw the reader through a novel almost as much as the story itself can. The question comes down to this: after I finish one page, do I want to read the next? Once the big-picture elements are in place, if the answer is still "not really," the solution can be to work on the prose.

How Line Editing Works

Line editing (also known as substantive editing) can overlap big-picture editing because it will stretch to include issues like characters who disappear partway through the book or scenes that lack credibility because of the way they are written—for example, if one character in a scene sounds just like the other character(s), or if a young character sounds far older than their years.

Line editing is also about paying attention to when information is delivered to the reader. How does a sentence or paragraph unfold? Do we see actions in sequential order or are they muddled? Removing confusion and clarifying action is a big part of any line edit. Ambiguity is fine; confusion isn't.

The objective of line editing is to improve the following issues:

- Poor flow (this might involve cutting or restructuring paragraphs or moving sentences around within a paragraph, a page, or a chapter)
- Continuity errors (e.g., a brown-eyed character's eyes become blue or a character who drives a Mazda suddenly drives a Subaru)
- Incongruities to do with characterization—this overlaps with big-picture editing (e.g., why a perfectionist would be sloppy with no explanation, or why a character would fail to use a useful object or skill, again with no explanation)
- Problems with setting (e.g., descriptions that don't work or details that create unnecessary confusion)
- Weak scene dynamics
- Issues of logic and credibility (e.g., someone drives across Russia in a day or high-level bureaucrats sound like high school students)
- Poorly constructed sentences and awkward phrasing
- Too little information
- Too much information
- Information delivered in the wrong order
- Character actions that unfold in the wrong order
- Word choices that draw attention to themselves and bounce the reader out of the story
- Overreliance on adjectives and adverbs
- Unintentional repetitions or ambiguities
- Unnecessary dialogue tags or attributions
- Not enough "beats" (actions) in a scene or, conversely, too many identical beats like shrugging, nodding, or sighing

- Not enough variety in sentence structure
- Clunky metaphors or similes

The Line Editing Process

Line editing begins with a very close reading of the text, during which I absorb the writer's style. It's a bit like playing someone else's music. Every paragraph, page, or chapter has an underlying beat or rhythm. When I'm line editing, I listen to that beat for a while. Then I join in, enhancing the rhythm by removing or rearranging anything that impairs its flow.

This is where I roll up my sleeves and actually make corrections and suggestions on the page, using Track Changes. For big suggestions, like reorganizing an entire chapter, I might use a comment balloon to highlight text to be moved to the next chapter, for example, or suggest that an unimportant or boring scene might be better delivered in a paragraph of narrative summary. I go through the novel this way, making suggestions, cutting or moving text, and proposing alternatives. Because I'm using Track Changes, nothing is actually changed until the writer comes into the manuscript and accepts or rejects each suggestion.

"Placeholder" text refers to new sentences that I write (sparingly), to either replace or elaborate on the writer's original text. These sentences provide the writer with a concrete example of what I feel is missing—more sensory details, better transitions, a "fuller" ending to a scene or chapter. The writer can use this placeholder text or can take another run at the sentences and paragraphs in question. The intent is to alert the writer to the issue, identify what's not working about the original, and motivate them to try recasting the sentence or paragraph.

When the full line edit of the manuscript is complete, I will often go back and reedit the first several pages, now that the rhythm is clear.

In a two-pass edit with line editing as part of the second pass, I do a bit of line editing on the first pass so the writer can see what it looks like. It's a way of letting them assess whether I'm in tune with the piece. If my approach is too heavy or too light, they can tell me before I do the entire manuscript that way on the second pass. If they like what they see in that first pass, then on the second pass I commit to the process wholeheartedly.

Line editing is a great teaching tool, one that can substantially improve a writer's prose in a short period of time. Once you have received good line editing, its value becomes crystal clear. Having my own writing line edited was a revelation as the extra words were stripped away, constructions like "there were" were replaced with clearer, stronger sentences, weak verbs were identified, and my prose became substantially better on every page.

Line Editing in Action

The following examples show some common issues that can be addressed by line editing.

WORDINESS

By wordiness, I am referring not to ornate writing but to using unnecessary words that weaken the reading experience. Wordiness has a cumulative negative effect on readers. For one thing, it's tiring to read and affects pacing and reader engagement in any genre. Over the course of a novel a few extra words in every sentence really add up, slowing down the reader's pursuit of the story, tempting them to set the book down, thinking they might try again when they're fresher. Once a reader puts down the book it's anyone's guess as to whether they'll pick it back up. The other big problem with unnecessary wordiness is trust. If you qualify and overexplain small moments, the reader doesn't feel trusted to understand. And if you haven't taken the trouble to carve each sentence into its best form, the reader might doubt your ability to tell a good story.

Wordiness is primarily addressed through cutting or recasting sentences. The idea is to remove unnecessary words anywhere they exist. This will give you room, both in the reader's attention and in the word count, for additional words at moments when the characters are having a deep experience.

Wordiness can manifest in any of the following ways:

- Editorializing
- Repetition
- Overexplaining
- There were…that and other unnecessary words

Editorializing refers to commenting on the action right after it happens. In other words, showing, then telling. Editorializing pulls the reader from the scene and we feel the writer hanging over our shoulder, making sure we get what just happened.

Example:

In the chaos of the storm, they did not notice her take the heavy golden icon from the saddlebag. ~~Ironically, her luck had not run out.~~

Repetition refers to saying one thing in two different ways. In the following example, the second sentence is more interesting, and it's all you need.

Example:

~~Spies were everywhere.~~ The director had eyes and ears everywhere.

Overexplaining comes when you don't stop at the end of a sentence, but go on with more words. I could have made that "when you don't stop at the end of a sentence." This sometimes comes from not trusting the reader to understand what you mean.

Example:

That bastard would take her grandmother's money and leave her homeless. She ground her teeth ~~at that disturbing thought~~.

There were... that and other unnecessary words don't add anything to the sentence in terms of stylistic oomph or reader comprehension. Sometimes, taking a leaner approach works better for the paragraph as a whole.

Example:

But there were giant sacks of money that they had hidden in surprising locations, as she discovered.

Better as:

But she discovered giant sacks of money hidden in surprising locations.

Or,

Example:

He pointed with his finger [nodded his head, shrugged her shoulders, squinted her eyes, thought to himself].

Better as:

He pointed. He nodded. She shrugged. She squinted. He thought.

Extra words don't have to be completely eradicated. Sometimes it works better for rhythm to use "He shrugged his shoulders." However, learning how to write lean will let your story shine. Once wordiness is reduced, the remaining elaborations mean more. The cumulative benefit to pacing and clarity will lead to a more satisfying and riveting reading experience overall.

This is not to suggest that every novel should have minimalist prose. Using more words than are needed can be a stylistic choice, and when it is, this choice should be respected. Writers like Stanley Elkin revel in excess. They digress, they qualify, they circle around a moment from many different angles, they dive deep into the character's consciousness and bring back gold. But what you might notice about Elkin's work is that despite the length and breadth of his sentences and paragraphs, there are no unnecessary words. The words aren't there through writerly inattention—on the contrary; each is needed, and each is carefully chosen to contribute to the overall effect.

PRONOUN/NOUN MISPLACEMENT

Sometimes writers use a pronoun at the first reference to a character in a paragraph, then switch to their proper name (Jane, say) for future sentences in the same paragraph. Because the proper noun is more distancing than the pronoun, this can give the weird effect of starting close, then moving out. Switching the noun/pronoun order so that the proper noun comes first in the paragraph allows us to move deeper inside the character's head as the paragraph progresses, which feels more natural.

Example:

She staggered and bent over with her hands propped on her knees.
Jane took in large, gasping breaths, as if she just had been sprinting.

Better as:

Jane staggered and bent over with her hands propped on her knees.
She took in large, gasping breaths, as if she just had been sprinting.

WEAK VERBS

Strong sentences use strong verbs. Wherever possible, have your verbs echo the scene's mood. The example below is from a gruesome and dark scene, so the proposed verb choice suggests adding to that mood via word choice that gives the reader more information on how the POV character is feeling. (This particular example also employs "There were...")

Example:

There were irregular bumps underneath the black fabric.

Better as:

Irregular bumps distended the black fabric.

OVERUSE OF ADVERBS AND QUALIFIERS

Adverbs tend to make prose purple and draw the reader out of the story. Be as sparing as possible with these. Sometimes what's really needed is a stronger verb.

Qualifiers such as "slightly," "sometimes," "sort of," "usually," etc. tend to weaken the sentence they're in. Natural in dialogue, at least for certain characters, but in exposition or narrative summary overuse of qualifiers can give the effect of weak writing.

"BACKLOADING" SENTENCES

Sometimes sentences reveal information on character actions out of chronological order—that is, the POV character acts and the reader doesn't know what is being acted on, or why. (In the following example, we don't know why she's prodding him with her boot until we get to the end of the sentence.) This can cause confusion and weaken the reading experience.

Example:

She prodded his shoulder with the toe of a boot when the steady shrill ringing failed to rouse him.

Better as:

When the steady shrill ringing failed to rouse him, she prodded his shoulder with the toe of a boot.

MUDDY OR MISSING TRANSITIONS

Missing or confusing transitions at chapter and scene breaks can create a gap in the reading experience if they aren't done well. The reader needs to be oriented in space and time, so we're not reading the scene trying to figure out where we are and who's talking.

WEAK PROSE IN POWER POSITIONS

Sentences at the beginning and end of chapters, scenes and even paragraphs are privileged, because the white space before or after gives them time to resonate in the reader's mind. Every scene and chapter, in particular, should end on a powerful note. Simply by moving a power word to the end of a paragraph you can create a better and more resonant chapter ending.

Here's a fun exercise: when you're done a draft of a novel, try opening a blank document and pasting in the first and last sentence of each chapter. It will tell you a lot about the reader's experience.

PROBLEMATIC DIALOGUE

Think of dialogue as a dance—it reveals character, moves the plot forward, and sounds real, although it's usually more interesting than the way people talk in real life. In some novels, dialogue can be pedestrian ("Hi, how are you?") or overly expository ("As you know, Bob, our mom is a surgeon.") Or it can raise credibility issues, for example when European characters sound like North Americans ("It's a blockbuster that'll rake in millions!"—said the Swiss computer programmer). Line editing will point this out and sometimes suggest different dialogue or encourage the writer to dig deeper into characterization to come up with a better version of the scene.

STOCK BEATS AND TALKING HEADS

By "beats" I mean pauses in the dialogue, wherein characters perform a gesture or examine each other's expressions. If beats in a novel are limited to nodding, frowning, or staring, or there are no beats, the scene can start to feel unrealistic. A stock beat isn't going to kill you occasionally, but if you use the same ones over and over, the reader can start to feel like they're in a very small room, bumping their head repeatedly against the ceiling.

Human behavior is quite varied. Writers can exploit that variation—not to draw attention to itself, but to create verisimilitude and strengthen characterization. For example, in a restaurant scene, stock beats might be sipping or chewing. There might be room for the characters to do other actions, ones more revealing of character or state of mind, like playing with their cutlery, shredding a napkin, or stealing the sugar bowl.

This is related to "talking heads." Sometimes characters exchange dialogue without doing anything else. This can work, especially for shorter scenes. But sometimes, stopping the scene's action while characters talk feels like an oversight—we forget where we are and suspect the writer has too. If a scene suffers from this issue, I might suggest giving the characters something to do together. It can be related to the conversation or not related—for example, a domestic argument while doing the dishes, or a love scene while bandaging up a wound. Or a love scene over the dishes and an argument over bandaging the wound. Having characters interact with the setting gives you more opportunities to reveal character and move the story, which can make for a more interesting read.

ISSUES OF LOGIC AND CREDIBILITY

Issues of logic and credibility usually come from failure to fully consider the reality of a character's situation. If writers don't imagine the scene well or don't do the necessary research, it shows on the page and this negatively affects how the reader feels about the book. These issues can range from factual mistakes like having a character saddle a horse wrong or drive east into the sunset, to bigger problems with motivations and plot events. Credibility issues can also come from failure to consider the cause-and-effect chain. If events in the climax require the protagonist to use a knife, laboratory, spaceship, etc., their ability to do so needs to be established earlier in the book.

The sole objective of substantive or line editing is to improve the reading experience by getting the heart of the writer's style on the page, uncluttered by problems. As with all editing, the overarching principle here is not to make unnecessary suggestions. And as with all editing, each suggestion is presented as just one solution to a problem. The value of line editing is that it shows the writer how to improve their own prose by alerting them to the fact that there's a problem and providing examples of how it might be addressed.

Working on the prose in this way will raise the novel up a level in terms of the reader's experience. It will also require time and imagination from the writer as they go through the suggestions and decide whether to take the option offered, leave the original as is, or come up with a new solution.

CHAPTER 9

What Copyeditors and Proofreaders Do

[A] copyeditor must read the document letter by letter, word by word, with excruciating care and attentiveness. In many ways, being a copyeditor is like sitting for an English exam that never ends: At any moment, your knowledge of spelling, grammar, punctuation, usage, syntax, and diction is being tested.

AMY EINSOHN

Copyediting is close, meticulous work that deals with correctness and consistency. It can also address some of the issues that line editing covers. Proofreading is a final step in preparing the book for publication. This chapter examines each in turn.

How Copyediting Works

Light, medium, or heavy copyediting means different things to different editors and different publishing houses. The tasks that are included in the scope of work can vary: some copyedits will include fact-checking or procuring permissions, while others won't.

Copyediting fiction includes the following tasks:

- Correcting errors of grammar, spelling, and punctuation
- Correcting errors in usage (e.g., words commonly confused, such as affect and effect, further and farther)
- Removing superfluous words that haven't already been removed by line editing
- Identifying and correcting or querying errors in continuity (e.g., changes to character names, physical traits, etc.)
- Identifying and querying errors in timelines
- Checking various manuscript elements, such as chapter numbers and the table of contents, for accuracy
- Consistently applying the chosen editorial style for abbreviations, treatment of numbers, and UK/US spelling

The Copyediting Process

Personally, because I almost always do a first-pass developmental edit or critique before engaging in line editing or copyediting, my process is a little different than a dedicated copyeditor's. I usually line edit and copyedit simultaneously, at least the first time through. Then I do two additional rounds of copyediting to catch anything I missed while I was caught up in line editing.

Most copyeditors who have not already line edited the document will need a couple of read-throughs of the manuscript to do their work effectively. It's almost impossible to catch everything in one read-through, and in longer works like novels, it's impractical to go through the manuscript a third time.

During the copyediting stage I read very, very slowly, focusing on one sentence at a time, looking for errors. As I read, I keep a list of things to look for on the next read-through—usually these are global notes about checking chapter or section numbering, style guide details, etc. I do this "first" copyedit on screen (it's really the second copyedit, because I have already copyedited as I line edited, but it's the first dedicated copyedit). When I get to the end of the document I run the software add-in PerfectIt, which is a great tool for alerting me to remaining inconsistencies.

Then I take a break if possible, to give my mind a rest from the detailed work. I look at my global list of questions and things to look up and make any final editing decisions, verify usage and spelling questions in the chosen style guide and dictionary, and consult additional resources if needed. (Personally, I don't offer fact-checking, but while copyediting fiction I will look into anything that doesn't feel right or that's inconsistent.)

Then I go back to the manuscript for the second copyediting read-through (some copyeditors refer to each read-through as a pass). At this point I will almost always print out the manuscript in "Final" or "No Markup" view so that I can't see my own edits, and mark up the hard copy. This lets me read the text with fresh eyes and makes it easier to catch additional errors and infelicities. I try to do this hard copy read-through on consecutive days, but without rushing through it. It's a quicker read than the first time through, but it's still slower than normal reading speed.

At this point I take the marked-up manuscript and enter its edits into the electronic file. After that, I run PerfectIt again to catch any remaining errors and inconsistencies. Sometimes I will use macros as well, to help speed up mechanical edits (e.g., removing extra spaces after periods). I run Word's spell checker and spot-check random pages. When the manuscript is as perfect as I can get it, I send it back to the writer with instructions on how to accept or reject changes.

When I return the manuscript to the writer it is covered in Track Changes. They must then go through and accept or reject each editorial suggestion. Because I do line editing and copyediting in one pass, I try to make it as clear as possible which edits are suggestions and which are obligatory for correctness and consistency. Even so, it requires focused attention from the writer to resolve all the queries, suggestions and corrections, one at a time. The idea is to end up with a clean manuscript, free of Track Changes, and pristine in its purity.

Many copyeditors offer a subsequent "cleanup" pass after the writer's been through the manuscript, to resolve any unaccepted edits and queries, copyedit any new text, and so on. This is a necessary step for publishers, but it might or might not be offered by freelance editors, depending on the writer's goals and the scope of work.

Since errors can be introduced after the manuscript leaves my hands, and since no editor is perfect, proofreading is a necessary final step, at least for self-publishing writers.

How Proofreading Works

After the copyedit, final revisions are made, and the manuscript is formatted for production. As discussed earlier, this is when the proofread happens. Proofreading is not a service all editors offer since it happens in the production phase. By that point, the editor has already done most or all of the other levels of editing for a particular manuscript, and is far too close to it to catch any remaining errors.

Proofreading is a systematic review of the manuscript that examines each page for errors and formatting inconsistencies or issues. Strictly speaking, it refers to examining final designed page proofs. These are the pages of the book laid out as it will look in print. If you are submitting to traditional publishers you won't have designed pages, so simply reading carefully through the manuscript or getting an eagle-eyed friend to do so will suffice. If you are self-publishing, you or your designer will have created an interior layout, which will need to be proofread before you submit it to the printer. Proofreading usually includes the following tasks:

- Examining the text and titles, pagination, and running heads for accuracy as well as consistency in layout and font
- Checking consistency of each heading level for font, spacing, size, position and capitalization
- Reviewing the table of contents (if there is one) and ensuring that the numbers match the page numbers in the text
- Examining each page to see that it looks good and is consistent in terms of margins and justification, vertical and horizontal spacing, widows and orphans (single lines at the bottom or top of a page), ladders (hyphens stacked like ladder rungs), rivers (gaps of white space running down a paragraph), paragraph indenting, fonts, etc. Ensuring also that odd page numbers are on rectos.
- Verifying that quotation marks and other punctuation are in place.

Those, then, are the tasks fiction editors perform. As you can see, they use many different skills and they require training, access to resources, and the ability to apply deep focus to the work. This type of work is not for everyone. If you find the tasks interesting, you can learn more about becoming a freelance editor in the appendix, So You Want to Edit Fiction?

The last three chapters have discussed how fiction editors work on novels. The next chapter discusses short fiction. The same processes apply, but with some adjustments for the shorter form.

CHAPTER 10

Editing Short Stories

S o far, this book has examined fiction editing in the context of its longest form, the novel. But editors also work on novellas, short stories, and micro fiction. The main differences among these forms are length and complexity. Because novels are longer, they can have more characters and subplots and can allow for more digressions, flashbacks, and shifts in point of view. Reading a novel is a much different experience than reading a short story.

What Defines a Short Story?

A short story is commonly defined as any complete story under 15,000 words. Novellas can range from 15,000 up to about 40,000 words. There's a gray area at either end of the novella word count range. If a manuscript is 15,000 words, is it a short story or a novella? And if it's 40,000 words, is it a novella or a novel? It isn't just word count that defines the novella form; it's also got to do with the coherence and focus of the narrative. Novellas usually take the reader through a specific central experience, often from a particular character's point of view, and with a satisfying resolution (not necessarily happy, but giving a feeling of completion). As to whether a work is a short story, a novella or a novel, there are no set guidelines to which everyone subscribes. The final arbiter is its writer and/or its publisher.

Super-short stories (a.k.a. flash, sudden, immediate, or micro fiction) are 1,000 words or less. Aesop's fables are one example. Yasunari Kawabata wrote 150 "palm-of-the-hand" stories between 1920 and 1972. *Esquire* magazine ran a column called The Napkin Project that included 250 short stories that fit on cocktail napkins.

Many publications and writing contests ask for stories between 2,500 and 5,000 words, possibly because in order to run a very long story, a publication must turn down two or three excellent shorter ones.

Why Get a Short Story Edited?

Writing a short story takes the same basic skills as writing a novel—you need interesting characters and a good story, or at least a good basic premise. Stylistic standards are very high at literary journals, so your prose must be excellent. Characterization, plot, setting, and scene dynamics are important. But novels can be a little loose, can wander down one path or another, and still be an excellent read. The smaller canvas of a short story means that every word counts toward its overall effect. There's no room for padding. And as you approach the very short forms, the usual material of fiction falls away—there might not be any actual scenes, or entire parts of the story might only be hinted at rather than put on the page.

Some literary journals get hundreds of submissions for each issue and might be able to publish only 1 or 2 percent of the stories they receive. In addition, they might see the same types of stories over and over and want something fresh. (This might be why so many journals ask writers to read prior issues—so writers can both get a sense of what's been done before and see how their own stories might fit a particular journal's aesthetic while being different enough to feel fresh to its editors and readers.) The result of these pressures is that the market for short stories is highly competitive.

Writers work with editors on their short stories for many reasons. Getting editorial help can be quicker and deeper than revising through trial and error or workshopping each story with other writers. Common scenarios include the following:

- Your story has been repeatedly rejected, but you still believe in it and want objective feedback on its weaknesses so you can increase its chances of publication

- You want to submit a story for inclusion in an anthology or literary magazine and know it needs polishing, cutting, or expansion to fit the submission requirements
- You want to enter a story in a particular contest and need to get its word count down
- You have several short stories and want to publish a collection. In this case, editing would not only examine each story, pinpoint strengths and weaknesses, and polish your prose, but also examine story themes and connections, and recommend overall order in the collection to create the most compelling reading experience.

How Short Story Editing Works

The editorial approach for short forms really depends on the form itself. On the long end of the spectrum, novellas can be approached much like novels. Novella plots are usually more streamlined or pointed, and the story thrust is, therefore, more direct. Character development often centers around one event, emotionally, and there's often less backstory and fewer POVs. But the processes outlined in the previous chapters for developmental editing, line editing, and copyediting are basically the same for a novella as they are for a novel. Novella editing can also take place over one pass or two—the first for big-picture edits and, if the prose needs work, a second pass on the revised manuscript for line edits and/or copyedits.

On the other extreme, very short forms—such as the drabble (one hundred words exactly), "55 fiction" (fifty-five words in ten sentences), and other micro-fiction forms—are rarely sent to freelance editors. Their forms are so restrictive that there's not much an editor can suggest that the writer wouldn't already know, and the cost of editing would probably far outweigh any financial reward from publication.

Short story editors should have excellent skills at both the big-picture and the line editing levels. They should be knowledgeable about the form and have relatively current reading practices that encompass literary journals or "Best of" anthologies. Each literary journal has its own style and preference—some like transgressive fiction, some ask for character-driven stories, some publish issues themed around subjects such as "work" or "risk." It can be difficult for writers and editors to keep up, and this is where anthologies come in handy, such as *The Best American Short Stories*, *The Pushcart Prize: Best of the Small Presses*, or *The O. Henry Prize Stories* (all published annually). For genre fiction writers and editors, there are anthologies such as *The Year's Best Science Fiction & Fantasy* and many others.

Ideally, the editor you work with will be an experienced reader of the form and familiar with the canon. It's even better if they have editing experience at a literary journal.

The process for editing short stories uses the same skills as novel editing, with some differences. Turnaround time is quicker because fewer words take less time to read. Sometimes all three levels of editing will be applied in a single pass, since it rarely makes sense to have a 5,000-word story edited for structure but not for prose. Sometimes line editing isn't really needed; many short story writers have already developed excellent prose skills. For these writers, story structure and emotional tone can be more of a stumbling block. However, since the cost of having a short story edited is low compared to the cost of a book-length manuscript, many skilled writers still opt for line editing, just to see what changes are being suggested.

When I edit short stories, my general approach consists of the following steps:

- Read the entire story, preferably in one sitting.
- Observe what the story makes me think about and how it makes me feel.
- Consider characterization—are characters well-drawn; do I care what happens to them; do I understand the situation they're in and why it matters; do they face obstacles; could any of the secondary characters be cut completely, or could two be conflated into one?
- Break down the plot, or sequence of events and choice of incidents. Many great short stories don't rely on plot to hold the reader's interest, but there is almost always a progression of events, even if it happens in a character's mind.
- Look at pacing and check if any parts of the story could be cut, either because they're unnecessary or because they detract from the overall effect.

- Identify any issues that take me out of the story world. Transitions should be effective and economical. Dialogue, description, and setting should work together to create an overall mood.
- At this point, I make initial notes about what works and what doesn't work at the big-picture level.
- Then I look again at the story's beginning—does it start in the right place; is the prose compelling? Because literary journals receive such a high volume of submissions, the acquisitions editors read hundreds of first sentences and first paragraphs. If these don't measure up, the editor won't get to the rest of the story no matter how good it is.
- I reread the story's ending—does it feel thin or rushed, or does it drag on; can it be shaped to intensify the mood, emotions, or thoughts that the reader experiences when they finish the story? Many stories don't have a three-act structure with a beginning, middle and end—for example, "The Solutions to Brian's Problem," a story of just over 1,000 words by Bonnie Jo Campbell, presents seven different and harrowing solutions for saving a baby from its meth-addicted mother. The main question is, does the story's form and structure work?
- If the structure is sound, then the final step is to line edit the prose. The goal of line editing, as with novels, is to draw out the story's natural voice, improve clarity, and remove redundancies or repetitions.

If I'm editing a story collection, I will do the above tasks on each story. Then I'll take a step back and start considering organizing principles for the collection. When a writer has worked on individual stories over years or even decades, it can be hard for them to see the collection as a whole. Juxtaposition (what each story follows and precedes) can create a particular effect even if the stories themselves don't change. Flow, coherence, and a sense of an overall arc are all affected by which story goes where.

When offering thoughts on a collection, I'll propose story order in the editorial letter rather than moving them around in the manuscript. Sometimes

I offer more than one suggested order and discuss the possible impact of each on the reader.

The edit is then sent to the writer. I include an editorial letter discussing the story or collection, giving organized feedback on what works and what needs work, and summarizing the recommendations for revision. The manuscript itself is attached, marked up with comments and line edits. Book maps and style sheets are rarely needed for one story but might form part of the scope of work for editing a book-length collection.

....

This brings us to the end of Part II. Now you know how fiction editors perform their magic. It is not that mysterious, after all. Editorial feedback should convince the writer that there's an issue while remaining open-ended or open-minded about how it might be solved. There is no one way to fix a problem. Whatever an editor says about your work should be backed up by examples or shown on the page, so that you understand the basis of the observation and can act on it with insight.

Part III provides information to help the practical writer save time, money, and energy in finding the right editor for their work.

THE PRACTICAL WRITER

CHAPTER 11

Time and Money

Being a fiction writer has always required a strange, stubborn persistence. Some writers are in the grip of full-on obsessions and want nothing more than to write for a living. Other writers have no interest in quitting their day jobs but write fiction because they find it interesting or fun to challenge themselves in this way. As a group, writers are used to working hard for months and years on the same story. They are used to turning down invitations in order to get through another chapter. They are used to the costs and consequences of writing fiction.

And just like everyone else, writers are used to paying close attention to the practicalities of life: what things cost, how long they take, and what they demand of us. After all, regardless of whether you intend to write for a living, every additional hour you have to work to pay for something is an hour away from doing the actual writing.

For self-publishers, e-books have made the publishing process relatively affordable, comparable to the cost of an annual vacation or a used car. But still, cost can be a barrier for many writers. There are plenty of fiction writers who never take a vacation and can't afford a car. So the cost of a professional edit might seem like putting money you don't have toward an enterprise that has no guarantee of success.

It *is* like that. In fact, it's exactly that.

This means that once you have decided to do it, you will want to get the most bang for your buck. You can do this by understanding how editors set their rates, keeping your publishing goals in mind, and having a plan B if all the quotes are too high.

How Editorial Rates Work

Editing is a service industry. The cost of an edit, like the cost of any service, is affected by a number of factors. These include the type of edit, the deliverables, the scope of work, the manuscript's word count, the quality of the prose, the turnaround window, and the editor's experience. For example, creating a book map for a novel can take eight to sixteen hours or more, depending on the story's length and complexity.

Professional freelance editors set their rates with the intention of earning a living wage. To calculate a freelance salary based on a living wage, one must consider not only the hours spent engaged in billable work but also factor in overhead—the time and money spent running the business: office rent, equipment, correspondence, scheduling, meetings, software, member-ships, professional development, website maintenance, and so on. Few professional freelance editors do nothing but edit. In a forty-hour workweek, they might edit for twenty-five hours and run their business for the other fifteen (these numbers are just an example and will vary depending on the business structure, whether it's tax season or year-end, how much time the editor spends marketing or updating their website or print materials, and so on).

Some fiction editors charge by the word, some by the hour, and some offer a flat project fee. Some editors will do rush jobs at a surcharge, some charge less for a longer turnaround time, others have almost no wiggle room in their schedules. Ten different editors might quote ten different prices on the same manuscript, with ten different scopes of work. Editors available through some third party sites, such as Upwork or Fiverr, might offer rock-bottom rates—as little as 200 USD for developmentally editing a 60,000-word novel—while an experienced editor might charge thousands of dollars for a developmental edit. Most freelance editors fall somewhere between these two extremes.

Some editorial associations post rate tables online. These can be a useful guide in estimating your project's cost, but they won't diagnose the situation for your particular manuscript, assign a level of editing, or give you a firm cost. Many editors post ballpark rates online, usually as a per-word or per-manuscript cost, along with the level of editing you can expect at each rate. I do this myself, but I never take on an editing job without seeing at least a portion of the manuscript, preferably the whole thing, to assess whether the level of editing requested is actually the level of editing needed.

The best way to find out what your edit will cost is to ask several editors to quote on the project. This is the sample edit. It's usually free, with no obligation to proceed. In a sample edit, the editor will comment on a few pages of your manuscript, do some line editing or copyediting, and write you a short proposal with their assessment of the manuscript's needs and a cost estimate for doing the work.

The purpose of a sample edit is partially to ensure that you get an editor who knows what they're doing and is a good fit for your writing, and partially to allow the editor to estimate how long the edit will take and get a sense of whether they'd like to work on your book. The only way for an editor to know that is to edit part of the text, track how long it takes, and develop an opinion on what level of editing the manuscript needs. Good editors won't tell you your work needs a particular level of editing without having first read a few pages.

Personally, when setting editorial fees, I almost always arrive at a flat fee based on the novel's word count and its readability (which includes everything from prose style to subject matter to characters to how well the manuscript's formatted). A flat rate is easier to work with because the writer knows up front how much it will cost. I will never come back for more money. This means that if the edit takes longer than I predicted, the writer benefits. If it goes more quickly than I estimated, I benefit. I always fulfill the editorial scope of work in its entirety, but what can sometimes make a project go faster are efficiencies of process and a laser-sharp focus. Sometimes an edit takes more time despite these efficiencies—if the issues are very subtle or if the manuscript devolves substantially from the portion I read for the sample edit.

Most editors will invoice in two or three installments and will take payment by credit card. Both of these practices can make a big difference to a writer's cash flow.

A note about cheap editors: The end cost of using an editor who charges way below the median rate can be higher than you might think. It's unlikely that an editor who charges rock-bottom rates will be a professional. And in the long run, paying an amateur is pointless since the work will either be done poorly or not at all.

One of my clients came to me several years after she'd started working on her first manuscript. I was the third editor she had consulted. Her first editor, referred through a university writing program, did a line edit without first doing a big-picture assessment. This editor gave up partway through, realizing that the manuscript needed better organization but being unable to offer practical help because developmental editing was not one of her skills. The writer found a second editor online. This person kept the manuscript for a year. When the writer finally got it back she found that the editor not only hadn't delivered the promised scope of work but had also added text that changed her intended meaning. Demoralized but not defeated, the writer then shared the manuscript with friends and asked for their feedback. The response was muddled and confusing. At this point, she felt "like a hamster on a wheel" and stopped working on it for a couple of years.

So a bad edit can be extremely disappointing and discouraging. And if you're not willing to give up on the book, you will still need to find a professional to fix the first editor's mistakes and do the work properly, costing you more time and money in the long run.

There will always be a range of quoted costs for editing a manuscript. The important thing is to find the right editor for your work.

Your Publishing Goals

Knowing how you will publish can help you narrow down what type of editing you need or even whether you need editing at all. If your goal is traditional publication, your story should be compelling and your manuscript should also be fairly polished at the stylistic level, but it doesn't have to be perfect. Depending on your strengths as a writer, you could be looking at big-picture editing, line editing, or both. You probably won't need copyediting unless your prose is very uneven or riddled with errors that interfere with the reading experience. Agents and acquisitions editors will notice if your manuscript is improperly formatted or contains many typos, but if the mechanics of your presentation meet basic standards (double-spaced, readable font, pages numbered, spell checked), no sane agent will turn down a manuscript they love.

Some of the manuscripts pitched to agents and traditional publishers don't need professional editing. The writer might be extremely talented, very experienced, have excellent beta readers, or just need no help. Even for novice writers, if the book's fairly well written and has a high-concept premise or possesses other qualities that make acquisitions editors want to buy it, there's no need for editorial intervention. If you are one of those writers, or your manuscript is one of those novels, congratulations—and I mean that sincerely.

However, since you're reading this book there might be a voice in your head telling you that you are not one of those writers yet—or rather, that this isn't one of those manuscripts. (Your next novel might be.) You might already know that literary agents and acquisitions editors will rarely give a novel they've rejected a second chance unless they have specifically asked you to revise and resubmit. That's why even writers who plan to publish traditionally might get editorial feedback on their novel either before they start pitching it or after they've pitched it to a dozen places with no success. This scenario is far more common than it used to be, primarily because traditional publishers so rarely accept manuscripts that need substantial work.

Writers who self-publish are completely in charge of ensuring that their work meets readers' standards. As a writer myself, I know how difficult it is to gain a fresh perspective on my own work. Another set of eyes is essential. But the level of editing you get is up to you. If you are looking for return readers, and ones who will refer your book to their friends, you want the story to be as compelling as possible and the writing as good as you can make it. That being said, even a light copyedit is better than no edit at all. Readers can attack like piranhas when they find a book riddled with typos or errors in grammar and punctuation, not to mention continuity issues or plot holes. So for self-publishing writers, the best-case scenario is that you have a budget for all levels of editing and that you connect with an editor who can provide all levels, at least for a manuscript or two.

Your Plan B

You might have seen this sign:

GOOD

FAST

CHEAP

PICK ANY TWO

For many writers, this states the problem in a nutshell. If you don't have a big budget, do you have to compromise on the quality of editor you engage?

Maybe. You do have to be realistic about what level of editing you want versus what you can afford. So if you have gotten a few sample edits and most of them quote double or triple the amount you have to spend, see where you might be able to cut costs. Here are some tips to help bring the price down:

Reduce the manuscript's word count. A 150,000-word novel will cost more to edit than a 75,000-word novel simply because it takes longer to read. If there are any scenes you were thinking might go, cut them now and ask for a requote on the new word count. (You won't get a new free sample edit, but many editors will come back to you with a revised cost.)

Reduce the editorial scope of work. You might want a detailed developmental edit with a book map, a revision plan, a video meeting, and a query critique, but if that's not attainable, then dial your wants down to a simple manuscript evaluation or critique—a more general assessment of where your story's at and what it might need. You'll get less feedback, which means more work at your end in revision as you will have to apply the suggestions without much direction. But if you are a fairly experienced writer and can think outside your own box, that will often be enough to set you on a meaningful track with your revision.

Be strategic about your spending and relate it to your publishing goals. If you're planning to publish traditionally, don't contract for copyediting or proofreading.

Lengthen your turnaround window by breaking the project into smaller steps and doing them over a longer period. This will give you time to save up and pay in chunks.

What if you can't afford an edit even once you have cut your wish list down to the bone? You can still increase the book's quality by self-editing, using beta readers, and employing some copyeditor "tricks" to eradicate most of the surface errors. The next chapter offers a more detailed look at how to get your manuscript into the best possible shape, either before or instead of working with a professional editor.

CHAPTER 12

The Do-It-Yourself Edit

Working with an editor might not be feasible. Even if it is, though, you'll save time and money if you self-edit your fiction first. This chapter looks at several approaches for a DIY edit. In an ideal world, you'd do all of the following steps to give your work its best chance of becoming a good reading experience:

- Self-edit first
- Use critique partners and beta readers
- Use copyediting checklists

The tradeoff for the DIY approach is that it's more time-consuming than working with a professional editor. It has the added problem of perspective— you might not be able to diagnose your novel's big-picture problems with plot or pacing, for example, because you're too close to see it clearly. However, no matter what your novel's particular issues are, following these three steps will not be wasted effort—you will learn a lot, and the story will become a better read.

Self-Edit First

If you really want to save money and get a higher level of editing, do as much work as possible on the manuscript before you send it out for sample edits.

Why?

You will get a higher level of editing. If the manuscript is relatively clean and free of problems you can spot yourself, your editor can use their time and energy for the work that only a professional editor can do.

You will save money. The less time the editor spends on your manuscript, the less it will cost you.

You will attract the best. The best editors want to work with strong manuscripts, just as the best coaches want to work with strong athletes.

So don't send a professional editor your first draft. Doing so will cost you more and get you less. Take the time to work out as many story problems as you can on your own.

Self-Editing Checklist

Following these steps will result in a better manuscript.

1.   When you reach THE END, give the story down time. Print it out, if possible, and put it away for at least a month. Schedule the date you will take it out.

2.   On the scheduled day, do a quick read. Make a list of first impressions—what strikes you about the novel? No more than a page, total.

3.   Write the sales blurb, jacket copy, or query letter. See if it reflects the novel. If it doesn't, that might be a sign that your basic premise is flawed or inadequate.

4.   Look into genre expectations. If you're writing a romance, is there a happily ever after? If not, what do you give the reader instead? (Literary fiction, perhaps?) If you are writing for a specific age group, is the vocabulary appropriate? Does the word count fall into publishing norms for that category?

5.   Assess your main characters. Who are they, what's interesting about them to the reader, and how do they change?

6.   Make a scene list, if you haven't already, to map out your plot. This can be as complex as a book map or as simple as a handwritten list of every scene from the novel's beginning to its end. Include the scene number, location (of the action), and a brief description of what happens.

7. Use the scene list to find turning points or doorway moments and ask yourself: can the scenes be rearranged to achieve greater drama or a more compelling flow? Does each scene earn its keep? Could they work harder to move the story, deliver information, or reveal character?

8. Use the scene list to map out the novel's cause-and-effect chain. If a scene has no cause and no effect, it might need to be cut.

9. In the manuscript itself, look at narrative modes and flow. Narrative modes in fiction include scene, exposition, and narrative summary. (For examples of the main narrative modes, see the glossary.) Do you use a variety of modes, or is it scene, scene, scene, scene? Would adding a bit of exposition or summary improve the pacing or flow?

10. Ask yourself: Do important moments occur in scene? If not, what is gained by rendering them via exposition or summary?

11. Examine and improve scene dynamics. What is the core conflict or tension? Do characters have short-term goals to keep the reader turning pages?

12. Polish your prose. Read prizewinning literary fiction on a regular basis. Each time you open your manuscript, take the opportunity to make each sentence in the section you're working on as good as you can make it.

13. Check flow and transitions between chapters and sections.

14. Read the novel aloud.

15. Get feedback from beta readers.

16. Do a final revision, run a spell check, and format the manuscript according to convention (double-spaced, twelve-point font, one-inch margins, page numbers, logical file name).

While it's true that a strong manuscript will save you money and get you a higher level of editing, editors don't expect a story to work on all levels when they get it. If you're planning to send the manuscript to an editor, do your best to make it good. When you've gone as far as you can, stop.

Use Critique Partners and Beta Readers

It is always a good idea to get free critiques before you pay an editor for a professional opinion. Critique partners are writers who are willing to read and give feedback on your manuscript (in whole or in part) in exchange for the same favor from you when their manuscript's ready. They read early drafts, pointing out big holes or problems. Because they're writers themselves, they might be better at honing in on why something is problematic in the reading experience. Before I became a professional editor, I swapped manuscripts with writers I'd met online or in person. I still do, with writer friends and members of my writing group.

Beta readers are non-writers who will read your novel and give you their opinion. Most of the time, they work for free, although a few editors offer beta reading as a paid service. (Be aware that professional beta reading is sometimes offered with the hope of upselling the writer to a higher level of editing.) Beta readers should get your most developed draft, rather than an early one. They should also ideally be avid readers, preferably ones who read in your genre.

The key to finding good critique partners and beta readers is creating relationships with other writers and with avid readers. Following are a few places to look for both:

Writing Courses

Take fiction-writing courses or workshops on a regular basis. Once you have gotten a sense of whether the other participants also write novels, work at your level, or have an interest in your genre, you can take one aside and mention that you are looking for a critique partner.

In-Person Writing Groups

A writing group that meets regularly can be a great source of support and critique partners. You can sometimes find these through local writers' associations (in my area, the Federation of BC Writers has a listing of local writing groups on their website) or through your community center or library. Some genre-specific writing associations (e.g., Sisters in Crime or Romance

Writers of America) have local chapters. Social media sites can also connect you to local writing groups.

If there are no groups in your area, you could start one. My writing group currently has five members and has been in continuous operation for about thirteen years. I'm the only original member left; our most recent addition was about a year ago. We don't set out deliberately to find members—what happens is that someone will leave, usually because they moved, and then weeks or months or even years later one of us will meet a possible replacement at a local workshop or conference. We invite them to come for a trial period to see if they are a good fit.

Online Peer-Review Groups

Online peer critiquing communities such as critiquecircle.com **or** scribophile.com can be a great way to find critique partners. These sites are reciprocal, which means you must also critique the work of other writers. Usually, there's a limit to how many words you can upload at a time, but if you develop a good rapport with one of your fellow members, you might exchange emails and enter into a mutual critique arrangement off-site, which would allow you to swap the entire manuscript.

Loosely Connected Acquaintances

Avid readers in your genre might enjoy the chance to help out a writer. Ask your friends and family if they know anyone who loves to read, and you might find a good beta reader.

Topic-Specific Clubs or Associations

Check out the local meetings or web associations for clubs related to your topic or genre. For example, historical reenactors might be into fiction about their particular era, or cinephiles might like novels about the film industry.

Treat your beta readers like gold. Reading and giving feedback on someone's novel is time-consuming. Even avid readers are used to reading traditionally published books, which have already been professionally edited.

Reading a flawed manuscript can become a chore that's hard to stick with if you're doing it on your own time and for free. To increase the odds that your beta readers will finish the manuscript in a timely fashion, you can bribe them with gift cards, wine, or other treats. This 'gift' can create a sense of social obligation that makes beta readers more likely to finish your book.

Let's say you have found willing beta readers. The next step is to give them your manuscript in either electronic format or hard copy. At the same time, give them a short questionnaire to complete. I usually ask mine to read the questions *after* they've read the novel, especially if the questions themselves might change how the reader encounters the work. (If you ask the reader, "Did it surprise you that Mr. Futch was Bella's long-lost brother?" then you've given away the story.) I sometimes enclose my list of questions in a sealed envelope, for hard copy readers, or email them with a subject line note asking them not to open the email until they've read the book. I don't expect any marginal comments or detailed feedback from beta readers, though sometimes my critique partners will provide those as well.

Here are some examples of questions for beta readers. You might pare this down to five or ten questions, and of course the questions will vary with the story:

1. What are your favorite and least favorite parts of the story?
2. Did you come across any issues of logic or credibility?
3. Where would you expect to find this novel in a bookstore or library? (This can illuminate whether your story fits its intended genre.)
4. Did you feel interested in what happened to the main character? If not, what stopped you from caring?
5. Were any images contradicted later on? For example, did you think someone was tall and find out later they were short?
6. Did you experience any confusion among characters? For example, did you wonder who someone was and have to flip back through the manuscript to figure it out?
7. Did you have a clear sense of time passing? Would you be surprised to learn the novel events take place over (say) three-and-a-half weeks?

8. Did the story feel complete? Do you feel anything has been a) left out or b) overdone?

9. Did you believe the details of setting? Can you think of any spots where there was too much description, or not enough?

10. Did you lose interest at any point? Could you tell me which page / chapter you drifted on, and why you think it happened?

11. Were any sections confusing, annoying, or frustrating? If so, which ones?

12. Did the end feel rushed? Or slow? Did it let you down? How would you have liked to see it end?

When you get feedback, thank the reader for their time and effort. You might not agree with their comments, but look for commonalities. If three readers say your character is unsympathetic or a certain section of the story had them drifting, take a good look at the issue and be prepared to rewrite. Ask questions if you have any and if the opportunity presents itself, but don't argue with your reader's feelings or opinions about your work. They probably won't feel valued and will be disinclined to help the next time.

Use Copyediting Checklists

Correcting surface errors can have a big impact on the reading experience, partly because it shows you care about the quality of your work and partly because the reader is less likely to be bumped out of the story.

Nothing can surpass a professional copyedit. But if that is not in your budget, use a copyediting checklist. You can find many excellent examples on the Internet, most of which will contain the following steps (the examples below are adapted from *Professional Editorial Standards 2016,* available through Editors Canada):

- Correct errors of grammar (e.g., lack of subject-verb agreement, misplaced modifiers), spelling (e.g., typos, homonyms, inconsistent hyphenation), and punctuation (e.g., comma splices, misplaced colons, incorrect apostrophes).
- Correct errors in usage (e.g., words commonly confused, such as *imply/infer,* and incorrect idioms).

- Identify and correct general information for accuracy (e.g., historical details, narrative timelines, calculations).
- Review organizational information (e.g., table of contents) to ensure it is accurate and correct.
- Identify and consistently apply your chosen editorial style (e.g., abbreviations, treatment of numbers, American/British spelling). This will be dictated by where you are publishing or submitting.
- If the manuscript contains foreign languages, apply consistency (e.g., capitalization, italicization, diacritical marks).
- If you're writing a series, consider developing a style sheet to record your decisions about style (as well as character names, physical features, and other information you'd like to track) so you can apply it to each book in the series without having to leaf through the original manuscript to see what you decided on. For an explanation of style sheets see Chapter 6.
- Recognize elements that require copyright acknowledgment and permission to reproduce (e.g., quotations) and apply for permissions.

Create More Distance

After you've self-edited, gotten feedback, and used a copyediting checklist on your manuscript, put it away again for as long as you can. Then spend a day or two where your sole objective is trying to see the text as though you are reading it for the very first time so you can find any remaining issues.

Sometimes I reformat my own manuscript landscaped in two columns and single-spaced. Then I print it out, guillotine the pages in half, hole punch them, and bind them together with zap straps (plastic ties), turning them into a crude little paperback. Then I take it to a couch and read it as though I didn't write it myself. It can be surprisingly helpful to externalize the novel in this way.

If you are self-publishing, you or someone else will need to proofread the final text once it has been laid out. At this stage, the more eyes you can have on the manuscript, the better. If you are proofreading it yourself, try the old editorial trick of reading it sentence by sentence from back to front, which will help you avoid getting caught up in the story.

....

You might not have the time or patience for all of these DIY editing steps. At a minimum, get feedback from beta readers, revise the manuscript at least once, and read the revised manuscript aloud.

At some point, you will put the manuscript down and say you have done as much as you can. If you think it's of publishable quality, you can start querying agents or go ahead with self-publishing. Or you can take the step of working with a professional editor. Where to look for one (and *what* to look for) is the topic of the next chapter.

CHAPTER 13

Seeking an Editor

When looking for an editor, you want someone with solid technical skills, knowledge of the publishing world, relevant educational background, and possibly experience in both writing and editing fiction. You want an editor whose abilities and sensibilities support your vision for the book. You want someone who will raise every aspect of your work to a higher level without compromising its soul. Finally, you want an editor who will do what they promise and will deliver the editorial scope of work for your manuscript on time and on budget.

The type of editor you work with will depend on a number of factors:

- Your writing style
- The novel's story world, plot, characters, and theme
- The novel's category and genre
- The manuscript's readiness and your experience level as a writer
- Your publication goals
- Your own assessment of the story's potential issues

It's important to get a good fit with your editor so you will trust their feedback and be able to distinguish between advice that resonates with your vision for the book and advice that doesn't.

You also want to find an editor who balances your strengths and weaknesses with their own. So if you're fantastic at plotting and telling stories, find a good line editor and copyeditor. And if your prose is gorgeous but your story engines tend to sputter out, find a good developmental or content editor.

Most good editors will be frank about their strengths and weaknesses. Just ask them and they'll tell you the truth.

From an editor's perspective, the search is a two-way street. So many people write fiction that good freelance editors often have their choice of projects and can book up weeks in advance. Personally, when I'm taking on a fiction manuscript I need to be interested in the characters and feel that the writer is in a position to act on editorial advice. This is another reason why many freelance editors do sample edits: it has to be a fit from both sides.

Sometimes writers switch editors, deliberately or unwillingly. Editors retire, get sick, change genres, or go to work for a publisher. Writers outgrow their editor or meet someone who's a better fit (not a better person, not even a better editor, just a better fit). Sometimes scheduling conflicts mean your editor is unavailable when you need them. If you begin your search with a wide net, you'll have a backup plan that may prove useful many years down the road.

Step 1: Create a Long List

Your first step is to do some research and create a long list of potential editors. Fiction editors can be found online, in person, and through referrals from other writers.

Referrals

This is the best way to discover a good editor. Most of my editing clients come through referral. One of my clients tracked me down after listening to a podcast where another of my clients described her experience of working with an editor. Others have recommended me to their writing friends. If you know other writers who have used an editor, ask them how it went. If it was a good experience, consider contacting the editor they worked with.

Or, if there's a published writer whose work shares a sensibility with your own writing, check the writer's website and see if they mention using a freelance editor. Since traditional publishing has coalesced into the Big Five, many former in-house editors have gone freelance. If there's a writer you love, go to the bookstore or library and find print copies of their books. Read the acknowledgments, where they will often thank their editor. Check the web to see if that editor's gone freelance. If they have, add that name to your list.

Online

Editorial associations provide membership to both freelance and in-house editors. The benefits of belonging to an association include access to training and resources as well as annual or biannual conferences and workshops. They often host a mailing list or forum for "water cooler" talk.

Membership in an association does not guarantee editorial competence, but it is a good indicator that an editor values their work and takes professional development seriously.

Some editorial associations are specific to a niche, such as academic or scientific editing. Others are broader based. The following three associations include fiction editors, and all three have online member directories:

- Editorial Freelancers Association (EFA): an American organization founded in 1970 and based in New York City, with over 2,400 members in the US and other countries
- Society for Editors and Proofreaders (SfEP): a UK organization founded in 1988 and based in London, with over 2,000 members, primarily in the UK
- Editors Canada: a Canadian organization founded in 1979 and based in Toronto, with over 1,300 members across Canada

To do an online search for editors, go to the organization's website, find their searchable database, and enter your criteria. (Note—some directories are more flexible and searchable than others.) Criteria might include skills (fiction editing, line editing, developmental editing, etc.), genres and sub-genres (literary, speculative, historical, romance, mystery, thriller, young adult, middle grade, and so on), educational and professional background, and even location, if you want to meet your editor in person

When you have searched for your criteria, a list of editors will come up. Read their profiles and note their website URLs. If they don't have a website, it could be a red flag that they don't work with individual writers or that they edit as a sideline rather than a full-time job.

As an alternative to the searchable database, some associations have "job boards" where you can post your manuscript's specifications and describe the type of editorial help you're looking for. The EFA, for example, has a free job posting service where you can describe the novel and ask for interested editors to respond. Be prepared to go through dozens of responses. If you take this route, go through the respondents as quickly as you can. Consider sending a form email (bcc) to anyone who doesn't immediately sound like a good fit. For the "maybes," you can go through the rest of the steps described later on, under "create a short list."

Since not all members of an association use the job board, many writers do both—search the association's database using their criteria and post their request on the board.

In Person

Writing conferences are a good place to meet editors in your genre. You can attend workshops and sessions that have editors on the panel or where the topic includes editing. For a guaranteed face-to-face meeting, you can sign up for "blue pencil" sessions if they are available. These are one-on-one meetings with an editor who has read a few pages of your work in progress. Blue pencil sessions are usually free. If you like that editor's approach, ask them if they do freelance editing. If they don't, ask if they can refer you to any colleagues. Finally, if you see a fellow delegate with "editor" on their name badge, try seeking them out at coffee breaks or lunch. Most editors are approachable and like talking about their work. They can be a great source of information, even if they don't do the type of editing you need. It goes without saying (but I'll say it anyway): be respectful of their time and energy.

Publishing Services Companies

If your long list is still too short (less than twenty names), consider checking Reedsy, Mediabistro or other go-between companies where fiction editors can be found. The more reputable sites have good screening processes, and you can find experienced editors on their lists. Other sites, like

Upwork and Fiverr, allow you to comparison-shop among service providers. Be careful if you use these sites since quality can be variable.

For self-publishing writers, companies such as BookBaby or Lulu offer editing along with a gamut of other services such as cover design, interior layout, International Standard Book Number (ISBN) registration, printing, marketing, and distribution. All these services come at a price. These companies do not make money by selling your book; they make money by selling services to writers. This means that your assigned "project manager" might be a customer service rep who tries to upsell you every time you call or email with a question. Also, keep in mind that some booksellers and libraries have policies where they will not order books with ISBNs registered to a publishing service. There's nothing wrong with this, as long as your expectations are clear and you know what you're getting into. These self-publishing services can be a good resource if you have the money and don't have time to put together a roster of à la carte service providers. However, if you plan to self-publish many books and want to control your own ISBNs, or if you don't want to repeatedly pay the company's markup for their services, then you might be better off spending a bit of time up front to find individual freelancers you can work with over the long term.

When looking at editor listings, job board responses, and online profiles, consider genre, experience, and the vibe you get from their testimonials and their descriptions of themselves and their work. Go with your instincts and make a preliminary long list of ten or twenty editors whose websites you will visit in the next step. It's worth developing a robust long list because not every editor will be available, be a good fit, or be interested in working on your fiction.

Step 2: Create a Short List

Take your long list of potential editors and spend a few minutes on each editor's website. The website can be a preview of their work style, including the quality of their editorial letters. You might want to create a spreadsheet or table to capture your findings. Consider the following when crafting your short list:

- Who are they? What do you like about how they present themselves, and what raises questions or red flags in your mind?
- Notice the website's **vibe and sensibility**. Is it text heavy and verbose, or clear and clean? Hard to understand, or written in plain language?
- Read the website's **definitions of editorial terms** to see what levels of editing they provide and what's included at each level. If they have no definitions or are vague, that can be a red flag. Some editors define their terms and scope of work more specifically at the sample edit stage, tailoring it to your project. But the website should have clear, basic information about what they offer.
- Read their **testimonials**. Notice the words clients use: insightful, blunt, detailed, helpful—these will tell you a lot about each client's experience. Testimonials can be faked, although I don't personally know of any editors who've done this. If you have any doubts, either don't include the editor on your short list or, when you get to the sample edit stage, ask the editor if they can give you the contact information for one or two previous clients.
- Notice what the editor says about **sample edits**. Some charge a fee, although they will usually apply that fee to the edit itself. Sample edit fees can be a problem from the writer's perspective because if you've asked for five sample edits and each person charges, you've spent funds before you even know who you're going to work with. If you don't want to do this, eliminate those editors who charge for samples.
- Note their process for **scheduling** manuscripts. Many editors book four to ten weeks in advance or longer. If your manuscript is ready and you're keen to move ahead, send a preliminary email to the editors with waiting lists and ask them about their current schedule. Sometimes an earlier opening is available if, for example, a scheduled client is not ready with their manuscript.
- Scrutinize their **About Me** page. An MFA in writing or teaching experience means they have technical knowledge and the ability to

teach or expand writing skills generally, as well as to give you specific feedback on your current manuscript.

- If they **write fiction** themselves, see if they have an agent and/or have been published. Being a good writer won't necessarily make someone a good editor, but they will know more about the querying and publishing process from the writer's perspective. If you're hoping to publish traditionally, this additional perspective can be both useful and comforting.
- Look at their memberships, and get a sense of whether they have a commitment to professional education.

Once you have eliminated editors who don't seem like a good fit, you should have a short list of three to five editors to contact for sample edits.

Step 3: Ask for Sample Edits

Many fiction editors won't take on a manuscript without doing a sample edit first. Depending on what level of editing you are asking about, in a sample edit the editor will read a few pages of the manuscript, line edit or copyedit a few hundred words, and send the writer their thoughts and the marked-up manuscript along with a quote and a recommendation for the level of editing they think is needed.

You might have met the perfect editor at a party, on a yacht, or through a friend. Still, ask them for a sample edit. Just because you get along in person doesn't mean they will be a good fit for your writing. And that is the purpose of the sample edit—it allows you and the editor to assess each other and determine whether you'd like to work together. It will also give you practical information about what working with a particular editor entails—cost, timing, process, and other important aspects of working with a freelancer in any field.

When asking for a sample edit, be sure to do the following:
- Be clear and concise.
- Give your manuscript's genre, title, and word count.
- Briefly mention your publishing goals.

- Say what type or level of editing you think you might need. (If you don't know, that's fine—the editors you approach will tell you what they think.)
- If the novel has already been edited, let them know that and say why you're getting additional feedback.
- Mention your timeline. If you are looking for an immediate turnaround, don't ask for a sample edit from editors whose websites say they are fully booked. Editors receive numerous requests for sample edits and each one takes time. If there's a clear mismatch in terms of availability, the editor would rather know that up front and save themselves the time of doing a sample edit.
- State your budget, if you have one. This will ensure that editors who charge more than your budget don't get mixed in with editors you can afford. If you don't know your budget or aren't sure, just ask for a quote.

Step 4: Assess Sample Edits

Within a week or so of requesting sample edits, you should have them back. If you haven't been edited before, prepare yourself for both positive and negative feedback about your writing. (If it's all positive, they might not be the editor you need.) Remember that the purpose of editing is to bring your story to its best possible form.

Review the samples by doing the following steps:

- Read each sample edit and compare what editors have delivered. This might include a section of the manuscript, annotated and/or line edited; a cover memo or email; and a quote for their services.
- Note how informative the cover letter is. How do you feel about its tone?
- Look at the manuscript itself. Do the marginal comments tell you anything you don't already know? Do they suggest specific solutions to problems on the page?
- Do you like the suggestions or think they're interesting?
- Do the line edits improve your prose without interfering with the novel's voice?

- Check the cover memo or email for a recommended level of editing and a proposed scope of work. In order to compare apples to apples, you must know what each editor is suggesting your book needs: developmental edit, critique, manuscript evaluation, line edit, copyedit. What, exactly, do they say they will do?
- Look at the quoted fee. Is it hourly, per word, or a flat rate? If it's a flat rate, check what that works out to per word. Editors who charge a lot less than the norm might not be experienced or professional enough to be worth the savings.
- Check whether they talk about the work process. Will the edit be done in one pass or two?
- Look at their payment terms. Do they charge a deposit to hold your place in their schedule? How do they invoice and how often? Do they accept credit cards or PayPal?
- Compare scheduling information and turnaround times. Do they give a potential start date and say how long it will take to do the work?
- Will they include a phone call to discuss the edit after it's delivered?
- Do they offer help with query letters or blurbs?

Step 5: Assess Your "Fit"

Look at the chain of emails that delivered the sample edit to your inbox. Each editor is a human being, and we all have different communication styles. Note responsiveness, professionalism, ability to answer questions clearly, sense of humor, warmth, or other personal qualities you appreciate. It's important that you trust your editor. If you don't like their tone or approach, or you find them flaky, unresponsive, or confusing, now is the time to remove them from your short list (but keep their contact information for the next step).

The question of "fit" goes both ways. Be aware that not every sample edit will result in a quote or an offer to edit the manuscript. Some editors work with new writers and early drafts, others prefer to work with more experienced writers and/or more developed drafts. Editors might decline to quote on a project if they feel that the novel isn't for them, if they think it isn't ready, or if their communication with the writer has raised red flags (more on those below).

Scheduling will be part of the fit. Turnaround time will depend on the following factors:

- The scope of work (type and level of editing)
- The manuscript's word count
- The manuscript's condition
- The editor's experience level and personal working style
- Whether the editor is providing one pass or two

Some editors work on one manuscript at a time and can turn around a pass very quickly. Others work on more than one manuscript at a time, usually at different stages, lengths, and genres. This works well because editing is incredibly focused work and switching from one manuscript to another (fiction to nonfiction, for example, or from a developmental edit to a final polish) can use different mental muscles and allow for a fully productive workday.

Most freelance editors will take between two and four weeks from the day the manuscript's received to turn around a book-length edit. For a very long novel, where the editorial scope of work includes identifying where it could be cut down to publishable length, another week or two might be needed simply to allow enough reading time.

Professional editors don't keep a manuscript indefinitely. They give a start date and a delivery date, and they stick to the schedule unless there's an unforeseeable calamity or serious health issue. If such a thing arises, they inform the writer immediately and set a new deadline as close to the previous one as possible.

Step 6: Choose Your Editor

You have received sample edits and compared them for quality, price, scope of work, and timelines. Now is the time to make a decision about which editor will be the right one for you and your book.

If more than one editor feels like a good fit, find a way to make a choice. This can be difficult, but it needs to be done if you want to move forward.

Sometimes it comes down to a simple thing like scheduling or cost. If you don't already know the answers, ask the following questions:

- When will you start work?
- If there are two or more passes, how long will each pass take?
- How is the second pass scheduled?
- What do you need from me, aside from the manuscript and deposit?

In the end, it might come down to intuition or a hunch that one particular editor is the right one for you. Always feel free to ask more questions or request a phone call if you're having trouble deciding. The worst-case scenario is that they will say no. The main factor in your decision should be how you feel about their work in the sample edit. If they met or exceeded your expectations and made you feel excited about working with them, they are probably the right editor for your work.

CHAPTER 14

Hiring an Editor

Here we are, in the land of commitment! In theory, you have self-edited your manuscript, gotten feedback from critique partners, researched editors, gotten sample edits and quotes, and chosen who you will work with. Now what?

Confirm

Contact your preferred editor and let them know you'd like to go ahead. If you have needs you haven't mentioned yet, do so now. Do you travel a lot and know that you might be unreachable for a period of time? Or do you need to discuss alternate payment options because you're unable to pay via their proposed system? Let them know that before they finalize their schedule and write the contract.

At this point, be sure to tell your other sample editors that you have decided to go with someone else and thank them for their time and effort.

Get It in Writing

Always, always get your agreement for editorial services in writing, no matter how much you like the editor or how brilliant you think they are. The editor should send you a contract or letter of agreement (LOA). The purpose of contracts is to remove confusion and manage expectations. Don't enter into any service agreement without one. If they don't send you one, ask for it.

The contract or LOA should be written in plain language. Review it carefully. It will likely include several clauses, such as the following:

Scope of Work

The scope of work details what level of editing will be provided and what type of feedback it will consist of. If there are two passes, each will have its own scope of work, often in the same LOA so the writer has all the information they need in one document.

Deliverables

Deliverables will usually include an editorial letter, the manuscript itself, and possibly a book map and/or a style sheet. Again, deliverables for both passes should be clearly stated.

Schedule

The schedule should include the start date, due date, and any milestones in between. If there will be a second pass, the LOA might also address how it will be scheduled.

Copyright and Confidentiality Clauses

Some editors will include these, while others won't. Confidentiality is about whether anyone else will have access to your manuscript, and copyright is about who owns the work. Some editors will assert copyright over the edited manuscript until payment has been received in full, at which point both versions (the original you sent them and the edited one containing their work) belong to you. Whatever their policy is, it should be in the contract or LOA.

Billing and Payment Details

If you are paying a flat fee, payment will likely be broken down into three or more payments: a nonrefundable deposit of 10–20 percent when the edit is booked, a 40–50 percent payment at the time editing begins, and a 30–50 percent payment on delivery. Be aware that some editors bill 100 percent before you see their work—half on starting work and half partway through.

If you are paying an hourly rate, the billing schedule should be clearly set out. There might be a cap, or the editor might have agreed to keep you apprised if the edit turns out to need more time (and, therefore, more money). The preferred method of payment should also be set out, and whatever billing information you need in order to pay the invoices should be provided.

Termination Clause

Every editorial contract should have a clause about what happens if either party decides not to, or is unable to, continue with the arrangement. Typically, the editor will return all edited and partially edited materials immediately. Depending on how much of the editorial scope of work has been completed, they may either invoice for any unpaid time or refund any time owed.

Other Clauses

Some editors might specify additional terms and conditions. For example, they might ask you to acknowledge that you (the writer) understand that editorial help does not guarantee successful publication.

A contract for editorial services is like any other contract. Read it, ask questions about anything you don't understand, and make a counterproposal if there's a clause you can't live with. Your job at this point is to make sure you understand its terms before you agree to them.

Pay Any Deposits

Because so much editorial work is done online with clients in other states, countries, or continents, most editors will use an online billing service (PayPal is one example) and will accept payment by credit card. Most will not schedule your manuscript or start work until the deposit has been paid.

Be Easy to Work With

I probably don't even have to say this, but professional and friendly behavior matters. Communicate clearly. Be responsive to requests for information. If you have questions, roll them up into one or two thoughtful emails rather than firing them off individually. Don't expect replies on the weekend unless that has been discussed.

Personally, most of the red flags I've encountered with potential clients fall under the umbrella of unprofessional behavior. The following issues can raise my antennae and make me think twice about working with a writer:

- Multiple disorganized or repetitive emails from the writer
- Unwillingness to answer questions about the book or provide additional information
- Complaints about pricing (as opposed to constructive ideas or a simple "sorry, it exceeds my budget")
- Worrying aloud (via email or on the phone) about how to pay for the edit
- An inability to use Word's basic functions to format the manuscript according to convention
- Sending the manuscript in multiple separate files
- Expectations that I will work weekends or prioritize their project over other deadlines if this hasn't been discussed and agreed to
- Late delivery of the manuscript without checking in first, or cancelling without notice

Some of these red flags (unfamiliarity with Word, sending multiple files) are not so bad, while others could have the editor pulling the plug on your novel. In general, if you treat the editor in a professional and friendly manner, you have nothing to worry about. Editors are people and they are pretty helpful by nature.

Being professional and easy to work with helps foster and maintain goodwill, which is part of what makes a strong relationship. It can also build collateral in the event of a future emergency—if, for example, you would like feedback on your query letter in a hurry or have a burning need for revision advice months or years later.

Professionalism doesn't mean you have to maintain a formal distance in correspondence or worry about revealing your true personality. Through your work, the editor might come to understand you on a deeper level than the people who see you every day. So you should connect with your editor. You should feel good about how they treat you. They should inspire confidence. They should have time for you, within reason. A good editorial relationship can be a match made in heaven.

Send the Manuscript on Time

Editors work to deadlines. If your manuscript arrives halfway through its editorial "window," this can set off a chain reaction for all the manuscripts booked after it. Sometimes that's okay; other times it creates hardship for the editor—they'll either have to rush through your edit or start the next writer's edit late. Rather than do this, editors might move you to a later slot, lengthen the turnaround time, or even cancel the edit and return your manuscript.

If you send the manuscript early, make it clear in your cover email that you know the agreed-upon start date and are sending it early to get it off your plate, or because you'll be out of town on the scheduled day, or whatever your reason might be. If you're going to be late, let the editor know as soon as possible and ask how that will affect the schedule and turnaround time.

Communicate Special Requests

Some style points are not set in stone, particularly for fiction. If you're getting a copyedit and you have specific preferences that haven't already been discussed (e.g., an alternate spelling you prefer, or no quote marks around dialogue), or if you know your own peccadilloes and want to ensure they are caught, send a short email or memo along with the manuscript, detailing your preferences. If it's a big-picture edit and you want extra help with dialogue, structure, or pacing, be sure to ask your editor to address those points in their critique.

Enjoy Your Break

While the editor is working on your manuscript, performing some or all of the tasks outlined in Chapter 5, take a deep breath, relax, catch up on your social life, or (even better) work on something else. Use this time away from the project to refresh yourself and to gain some distance. The more distance you can create, the easier the revision process will be.

CHAPTER 15

After the Edit: What Now?

*The author receives the editorial letter and possibly
goes into shock. He or she has worked so long over
the manuscript, fixing and polishing, maybe showing
it to friends for comment, until it seemed perfect. Now
it has suddenly become the equivalent of a first draft.*

RUTH CAVIN

It can be nerve-wracking to see your editor's email in your inbox, waiting to be read. You might click on the email and download the files with trepidation, wondering just how much work they're suggesting you do.

First, send the editor a quick note to acknowledge receipt of the files.

Don't rush into tearing the manuscript apart. Approach it systematically. Be sure to practice good version control. Open the manuscript to make sure you can read the comments and Tracked Changes, then save it as a new file, in a logical folder, with a logical name, possibly including the date or a version number.

Following a big-picture edit (developmental edit, critique or manuscript evaluation), download the editorial letter and read it at least twice. Get acquainted with what the editor's suggesting. This can be an emotional experience as you realize that what you thought you did wasn't quite on the page. Be brave.

The editorial letter should not be so demoralizing that it puts you into an emotional tailspin or causes you to become paralyzed and unable to start revision. In fact, it should energize you and incite your enthusiasm for going back into the book. A good editorial letter can be one of the best experiences of a writer's life. There is nothing more exciting than seeing a reader's perspective on your novel—an informed, intelligent reader with the tools and skills to analyze your story and tell you about their experience, to say what they loved, to identify holes and suggest ways to fill them, to see what might be cut and demonstrate how it will strengthen the book, turning your novel into something the reader can't put down.

If the deliverables include a book map, read it once or twice. Book maps dissect structure particularly well and will give you another lens on the manuscript and the revision.

Finally, open the manuscript again. Go through it and read the marginal comments, making notes for yourself as you go.

By the time you have gone through all the documents, you will have assessed the extent of the work required. Now, develop a revision plan. You might write out the plan step by step, both to feel more in control of the situation and to give yourself something to check off as you work your way through revision.

The editorial letter might suggest an entry point for the revision, but how you revise is a personal decision that will take into account your thinking style and your tolerance for mess. Some writers work their way through the book from front to back. Others do a separate pass for each issue: one for moving scenes around, one for dialogue, one for setting, one for POV transitions, and so on. Changing a character's arc will probably mean writing new scenes or deeply revising existing scenes. The main idea is not to panic at the amount of work to be done but to just take it one step at a time.

Revising a novel can take weeks or months. As you work, remember your original vision for the book. Editors can make suggestions but they're not the ones trying to make them work. A good editor will explain the effect of making a change—they'll often make a persuasive case, especially for big-picture suggestions that require a lot of work. But it's the writer's job to assess whether these suggestions make sense. Editorial comments can spark a new inspiration, with the result that the writer chooses to neither take the advice nor reject it outright, but try something else.

You don't need to take all the advice an editor gives because the novel always was and always will be your own creation. But a good edit can bring your work to an entirely new level and can change your writing life. Seize the opportunity with both hands and take the feedback seriously.

On a similar tack, it's always good to think about how an effect might be achieved with changing as little as possible of the work you've already done. This is not only to save energy, but also because what you have in a manuscript can be thought of as a gift from an earlier self, if you will, and some juicy stuff might be lost if change is attacked with too much gusto.

Be aware that during revision, if a manuscript has serious structural or plot issues, the editor's marginal comments might become less and less relevant as you work your way through them and scenes are stripped down, expanded, moved, or cut completely.

If a second pass is included in the editorial scope of work, do your best on the manuscript's big-picture issues, then send it back to your editor for line editing and/or copyediting.

Following a line edit or copyedit, the manuscript will be covered with redlining (edits made with Track Changes), showing all the changes made. This is when you have the opportunity to accept or reject the editor's suggestions. To see what accepted edits will look like, you can toggle to the final view to read the text as if you've accepted the edits (instructions for this will vary depending on which version of Word you have). Then you can go back into the marked-up view, put your cursor on the edit, and accept or reject the change by right-clicking your mouse.

Line edits and copyedits can be a pain to go through since many of them are small and hard to see. The easiest way to see them is to magnify the manuscript by using the slider bar along the bottom right of your Word screen. Another way to see copyedits more clearly is to reveal the formatting (paragraph breaks, spaces, etc.). Any time there's a black vertical line on the left margin, that means there's a suggested edit that hasn't been accepted.

In reviewing copyedits, be aware that a human being performed the work. Editors are perfectionists, and they are helped by macros and specialized software, but perfection is so far unattainable by humans. So after you have gone through the copyedit and accepted or rejected the redlining and suggestions, you will still need to have someone proofread the final text— either yourself, an eagle-eyed friend, or a professional proofreader.

If your editor offers a post-edit phone or video meeting, take them up on it, even if you don't know what you're going to say. An editorial letter, no matter how detailed, can't give you the back and forth of an actual conversation. A half-hour phone call can give you one or more "aha" moments about your story and about how to approach the revision. Asking questions is good—either about something you didn't quite understand, or to get more advice on where to start revision. Prepare the questions ahead of time and ask the editor's permission to record the phone call—most won't mind.

In addition to help with the manuscript itself, you might be looking for help in understanding or navigating the publishing industry. You might want an assessment of your query letter or wonder if the editor knows any good cover designers or has any idea which agents you should approach.

Be courteous regarding requests for follow-up help. Some editors may include a quick look at query letters or give basic advice on how to approach agents as part of the edit. Others charge an hourly rate for additional services or don't offer them at all. If you aren't sure, ask.

Evaluating the Edit

Take some time to reflect on your experience after an edit. Was it helpful? Did it give you a way back into revision? Was it more than you expected, or less? Did you get your money's worth?

If you liked your editor's work, consider saying so in writing. Offer a testimonial for their website or tell your writing friends. If you're submitting to publishers and don't want it generally known that you've gotten professional help with your manuscript, your testimonial can be anonymous.

Keep your expectations realistic. A good editor can identify issues and suggest what to do. A very good editor who's also a writer can show you how to do it. But the editor can't rewrite your book for you. In the end, each edit is only as effective as the author's willingness to revise.

What if you got a bad edit? Did your editor misrepresent themselves or their abilities? Did you spend all that money and time only to get back a manuscript that's in worse shape than it was before, except in different ways? Editing is not usually the type of work people take on with the intent of evil-masterminding their way to world domination, but bad editing happens, and scams have been known to exist. One example is EditInk, a kickback referral scheme in the mid-1990s whose perpetrators were sued by the New York State Attorney General for deceptive business practices, false advertising, and fraud.

With the growth of self-publishing has come a rise in amateur editors, and although they might not be deliberately ripping off writers by delivering poor work, the end result feels the same. Bad editing can stem from the editor not understanding their role, not having sufficient training or a strong enough reading sensibility, or not being able to discriminate between expressing their personal biases and doing what's right for the book. It can come from ignorance (for example, changing "hansom cab" to "handsome cab" because they didn't know hansom cabs existed, or inserting errors due to ignorance of the rules of grammar, spelling or punctuation). It can come from not understanding the story itself, or from trying to impose their own vision on it (for example, suggesting you change your protagonist from a man of forty to a boy of nine). In case you're wondering, these examples come from real life.

Bad editing can also happen in the interaction between the writer and the editor, and might stem not from inexperience but rather from hubris or disorganization. If the editor's inaccessible, won't answer questions, doesn't explain the rationale for changes that seem arbitrary, takes far longer than they said they would, or delivers anything less than what was promised in the contract and scope of work, it turns into a bad experience for the writer.

What can you do with a bad edit? First, be absolutely sure that you're right. Not liking an editor's advice is not the same as not liking their work—if they fulfilled the contract, they have done their job. But if something wasn't delivered or was done so badly that you'll have to pay to get it redone, contact the editor, tell them what you want, and ask what they would like to do about it. If they are unresponsive and you are ready to consider legal action, consult a lawyer.

But the best way to deal with bad editing is to do due diligence before you hire an editor. You can do that by getting sample edits, paying attention to credentials and testimonials, carefully reviewing the contract for details regarding scope of work, schedule, and deliverables, and ensuring that expectations are clear and any lingering questions about what you will get are answered before work starts. If you have doubts at the hiring stage, listen to them and go with another editor.

Learning from the Edit

The nature of editorial feedback will tell you about your weaknesses as a writer. Take some time to analyze the overall nature of the editor's suggestions. Even if the editorial letter isn't a model of clarity and comprehensiveness, you can learn a great deal from studying the manuscript itself. For example, if the text was line edited, what types of suggestions were made? Were they cuts or additions? I once got several chapters of a novel line edited and when I analyzed the edits, I discovered that out of ninety suggestions, only one requested more information in a sentence, for clarity. The other eighty-nine suggested cutting extra words, for elegance and flow.

Take a really close look at any line edits and copyedits and ask yourself what they tell you about your writing tics and habits. Aside from stylistic choices, try to assess what kinds of things triggered suggestions by the editor. Were there random shifts in tense or frequent corrections to comma placement? Was your writing inattentive, with weak verbs or overuse of adverbs? Did your sentence structure lack variety? Did you overexplain character movements? Did you habitually construct sentences with actions unfolded out of chronological order? Was there frequent unintentional confusion or ambiguity?

At the big-picture level, the editorial letter should point out the manuscript's major weaknesses. But you can also find this out by going through the manuscript itself (that is, if your editor includes marginal comments), and spending some time analyzing the editor's reactions on the page. If there are tons of comments about scene dynamics, those will merit extra attention when you're going through your next revision or writing a new novel. If there are questions or comments about cause and effect or about what's at stake overall, there might be a need for more braiding of story threads, perhaps to do with the evolution of your story world.

Using editorial feedback analytically to learn more about yourself as a writer gives you the insight to gradually chip away at your blind spots. Then, through attention and effort, you can begin to turn your weaknesses into strengths. You might still have trouble with writing projects; they could still drive you crazy at times, but you won't be repeating the same mistakes over and over. As each weakness is addressed and overcome, new ones emerge. It could take ten years of steady writing to become a very good writer. But once you've done the work, your level of ability will be high. And this will serve you well for anything you care to write, in any genre, for the rest of your writing life.

Last Words

Even the most successful writer lives out on a limb.
It's a deeply risky and precarious way to live. It can
be equally thrilling and demoralizing. It's life on a
high wire and there is nothing like it: creating
original work. Making something out of nothing,
pulling rabbits from hats. However much power it
feels like the publisher has, it's the writer, ultimately,
who has the power to create.

BETSY LERNER

You hired an editor; they did a good job. You got clarity about your manuscript and learned how to be a better writer. You took the time necessary to revise the work. Now you are sure your novel is ready to start its journey toward readers.

It almost goes without saying that getting a novel professionally edited does not guarantee its success. Your book could be the best possible version of itself, and it still might not sell. Many factors are involved over and above the work itself.

If your novel doesn't sell after a professional edit, has the edit been a waste of money? That depends on your perspective. If you learned something from the editor, if you became a better writer, and if you can apply what you learned to your next book, then it wasn't a waste.

Most writers know that writing is not all sunshine and lollipops. Being a fiction writer forces you to use all of yourself, and this makes for a better and more interesting life. But it's not easy. If it were easy to write a novel, everyone would do it.

Even if you don't get a publishing deal or self-publish your writing, you can still put your work out into the world. Seek your readers by any means available. Sign up for readings, submit your stories to contests, put them up on the world wide web, join writing communities, and swap your work for critique. Develop your writing practice and tweak it whenever you need to in order to keep the words flowing. Be free when you write and ruthless when you revise. Keep working on your craft.

Publication might not happen the way you pictured it, it might take longer than you thought possible, and it might require sacrifices and compromises you didn't expect. But if you persist—learning as much as you can, writing as much as you are able to, and producing the best work you are capable of— you will move closer and closer to successful publication. Then one fine day, readers you've never met will hold your book in their hands, take it to the cashier, buy it online, or ask their librarian to stock it. They will read it, love it, review it, and recommend it to their friends.

For the rest of your journey toward publication, I wish you resilience, persistence, and good luck.

So You Want to Edit Fiction?

For anyone considering becoming a fiction editor, the first requirement is a highly developed reading sensibility. You must be an experienced, fluent, and thorough reader, whether in general fiction or in a specific genre. It's even better if you write fiction yourself, belong to a writing group, and have been told that your critiques are useful. These are all good signs.

The editing sensibility can't be taught, but if you have it, then the rest of what's needed can be mentored and nourished into the required skill level. Join an editorial association and read their group forums or mailing lists. Attend conferences and listen to podcasts featuring editors. Take webinars and online courses. Read the books mentioned in the bibliography.

In particular, be sure to read two excellent essay collections—*Editors on Editing*, edited by Gerald Gross, and *What Editors Do,* edited by Peter Ginna. These books offer interesting glimpses into editorial sub-specialties and give great insight into the editorial field as a whole: its purposes, preoccupations and challenges. I also recommend Thomas McCormack's idiosyncratic and entertaining book *The Fiction Editor, the Novel and the Novelist*, first published in 1961 and re-issued in 2006, which offers one editor's approach to editing fiction.

Education and Training

Part II of this book has given you a good basic approach for editing any fiction manuscript. You could try it out on a friend's manuscript and see how it works.

However, if you want to make a living as an editor, you will need additional training in the form of editing courses and/or mentorship or instruction. Many excellent editors have been trained and mentored at publishing houses. An MFA in creative writing is also good training for being a fiction editor. By the time you have completed an MFA you will have gained a solid understanding of craft, read hundreds of excellent novels and taken them apart, written your own novel or story collection, and had it critiqued by professional writers and writing teachers.

But you can most certainly edit fiction without an MFA and without having worked in traditional publishing. Courses on fiction editing are available from the Editorial Freelancers Association, the Society for Editors and Proofreaders, and Editors Canada. Some universities and colleges also offer editing certifications. Publishing programs can be found at both the undergraduate and graduate level, and their offerings usually include editorial training. Take as many courses as you can afford—first a basic course that shows you how to edit all prose, then additional courses on editing fiction. If you can find an editor who is willing to mentor you, or an editorial services firm that will provide training or internship, even better.

Wherever you get your training, you'll need to see examples of a good editorial letter for each level of editing, and you'll need to learn how to write clearly. You'll need to get feedback on your first few edits. Ideally, you will have had your own writing edited at all levels as well.

The Business End

In practical terms, you will need at least one reliable computer (PC or Mac) with Word and Excel, a business name and email address, and a way for fiction writers to find you (a website and online profiles). You should have a good dictionary, thesaurus, and style guide, as well as any additional reference books you discover along the way. You'll need a way to manage projects and track your time so you can give accurate estimates for how long an edit will take. (For example, if you know that it takes you sixty to ninety hours to do a two-pass edit of a 90,000-word novel, you are far less likely to undervalue your work.)

If you can't or don't want to work for a publisher or a book packager, you will also need to develop the skills and abilities to run a business. These skills fall into the following broad categories:

- Getting the work (e.g., marketing, performing sample edits, preparing quotes, and writing contracts)
- Doing the work itself (e.g., exercising strong editorial skills, excellent writing skills, and solid project and time management skills)
- Running the business (e.g., invoicing; accounting; purchasing templates, tools, software, and other technology; and participating in professional development activities)
- Growing the business (e.g., developing and selling a variety of editorial services; potentially hiring, mentoring, and managing other staff; and potentially teaching)

All aspects of running a business require good communication skills. The same applies to fiction editing. Writers and their work must be treated with respect, but at the same, time your feedback must be utterly honest. There can be no waffling about what works and doesn't work. Similarly, there can be no waffling about contracts, invoices, and the myriad details involved in operating as a professional. If this doesn't appeal to you, don't do it. Writers don't want to work with freelance editors who are struggling with the basics of project management or business communications. You would be better off interning with a publisher or finding another way into the editing world.

The Editing Life

Editing professionally is a challenge that takes energy, commitment, and the ability to thrive on uncertainty. In the first few years, you might need a nest egg or an investor to fill in any gaps in earnings while you master the learning curve. It also takes an ability to manage stress. Because it's a deadline-oriented service, you get used to living with the reality that there is always more work you could be doing. In the early years of a freelance editorial business, holidays can be short or nonexistent, and there can be many late nights at the computer as you learn how to schedule and balance your workload.

The rewards are huge. Editing exercises all of your faculties: you're an analyst, a creator, a midwife, a source of information and encouragement, and a teller of truth. You get to read books all day long, work with writers who are hungry to improve, and contribute your skills and abilities toward helping these writers get their work out into the world. And to a book lover, what could be better than that?

Glossary of Terms

B elow are definitions for some of the literary and editorial terms used in this book. For a more in-depth look at editorial terms, see an excellent small book called *The Editor's Lexicon: Essential Writing Terms for Novelists*, by editor and writer Sarah Cypher.

acquisitions editor: An editor at a publishing company who reads incoming manuscripts and decides whether or not they are a good fit for the publisher. Also called an acquiring or commissioning editor.

act: A unit of structure in the novel. Three-act structure at its most basic consists of beginning, middle, and end.

advance: A sum paid to the writer in advance of royalty earnings. Royalties are credited against this advance and kept by the publisher until the advance is earned out, after which royalties start going to the writer.

agency: The character's capacity to act or exert power and be the driver of events.

agent, literary: A professional who represents the writer's work to publishers and negotiates on the writer's behalf.

Amazon: An online vendor of books, toys, clothes, electronics, music, videos, and other creative content and consumer goods. In effect, a giant search engine that can connect potential readers to your book.

antagonist: The character (or situation) that contends with or opposes the protagonist.

arc: How a character develops or changes over the course of the story. Since characters create plot, arc can also refer to how the plot develops.

backstory: Information about the characters' lives before the novel began.

beta reader: Also known as a "first reader" or critique partner. A person recruited by the writer to read their manuscript and provide feedback, usually for free or on a reciprocal basis.

Big Five: As of the writing of this book, these include publishing houses Penguin Random House, Hachette Book Group, HarperCollins, Macmillan, and Simon & Schuster.

big-picture edit: Addresses holistic aspects of the novel (structure, plot, characterization, pacing, etc.). Also known as a content edit, a developmental edit, a critique, or a manuscript evaluation. See Chapters 5 and 7 for more detail.

BISAC (Book Industry Standards and Communications) codes: Standard alphanumeric descriptors agreed upon by the Book Industry Study Group and used for categorizing books.

blurb: Can refer to the book's back cover promotional copy, a quote from a review, or a prominent person praising the book. Blurbs appear on the book's cover, usually the back.

book doctor: a developmental editor who works with the writer to completely overhaul a struggling manuscript, often suggesting substantial structural changes that require extensive rewriting.

book map: A grid or table that analyzes your novel's structure, plot, themes, braiding, and/or POV. See Chapter 6 for more detail.

braiding: Editor Thomas McCormack, in *The Fiction Editor, the Novel, and the Novelist*, refers to braiding as the degree to which a character's actions and motivations interact with those of other characters, spurring the story toward a satisfying enmeshment. Characters whose stories don't braid can give a novel an episodic feeling or a lack of momentum, since any rise to a climax will be experienced by each character alone. McCormack points out that when novels with multiple separate storylines do succeed, it's often because each character is reacting to a shared "situational energy-source," like the bubonic plague.

category: The descriptor or numerical code that tells vendors and libraries where to place your novel (e.g., Juvenile fiction/Dystopian). Relates to BISAC codes.

characterization: How a character is portrayed to the reader.

climax: The point of highest dramatic tension.

comedy: The story of a character's rise, often through personality assets.

comments: In Word, a review tab function that allows a reader to insert marginal comments in an electronic document.

commercial fiction: Popular and entertaining fiction that encompasses all of genre fiction, including subgenres such as mystery, romance, science fiction, fantasy, horror, etc.

concrete: Characterized by or belonging to immediate experience; naming a real thing.

conflict: The opposition of persons or forces that gives rise to the dramatic action in a novel.

copyedit: Also spelled as two words: copy edit. Corrections to the spelling, grammar, and punctuation of a written work, with the objective of applying consistency and ensuring correctness. See Chapters 4, 5, and 9 for more detail.

critique: A type of big-picture edit that provides an overall assessment of the novel's strengths and weaknesses and suggests areas to focus on in revision. Addresses holistic aspects of the novel (structure, plot, characterization, pacing, etc.). See Chapters 5 and 7 for more detail.

crucible: A situation or place that keeps the characters together during an ordeal in which concentrated forces interact. Their motivation to stay is greater than their motivation or ability to leave.

denouement: The final outcome of the novel's main dramatic complication.

developmental edit: A type of big-picture edit. Addresses holistic aspects of the novel (structure, plot, characterization, pacing, etc.). Can be done on a work in progress or early draft as well as on completed manuscripts. See Chapters 5 and 7 for more detail.

dialogue tags: Also called attribution tags. Words that identify the speaker and either follow or precede the line (e.g., "he said").

diction: Choice of words.

distribution: The process of getting books to consumers, whether physical or electronic.

e-book: A book published in electronic form.

episodic: Events in the story seem randomly placed, without integration into the novel's cause-and-effect chain, not building to a climax.

exposition: Explanatory prose that gives the reader the information needed to understand the story. Writing that informs, explains, or describes. For example:

> John Reed was a schoolboy of fourteen years old; four years older
> than I, for I was but ten: large and stout for his age, with a dingy and
> unwholesome skin; thick lineaments in a spacious visage, heavy
> limbs and large extremities. He gorged himself habitually at table,
> which made him bilious, and gave him a dim and bleared eye and
> flabby cheeks. He ought now to have been at school; but his mama
> had taken him home for a month or two, "on account of his delicate
> health."
>
> Charlotte Brontë, *Jane Eyre*

flash fiction: A type of very short fiction.

flashback: A scene or scene fragment set earlier than the story's beginning.

Freytag's Triangle: Pyramidal diagram by German writer Gustav Freytag (1816–1895) that explains dramatic structure in five parts, with three crises. Freytag's Triangle is often used as a teaching tool.

genre fiction: Novels intended for a specific popular audience, fitting into existing categories such as mystery, science fiction, etc.

hybrid author: A writer who publishes some works traditionally and self-publishes others.

hybrid publisher: A publisher who provides paid services directly to writers.

immediate fiction: A type of very short fiction.

independent (indie) publishers: Can refer both to independent publishers (usually smaller firms) who put out work by a number of writers and to writers who self-publish only their own work.

International Standard Book Number (ISBN): A unique ten- or thirteen-digit number assigned to each format of a published book (e.g. electronic, paperback, hard cover, audio).

irony: The result of a difference in point of view or values between the character and the narrator, of which the reader is aware. Dramatic irony happens when the reader knows something the character doesn't, or vice versa.

line edit: A level of editing that works on prose at the sentence and paragraph level. Gives stylistic feedback while retaining the work's voice. Improves flow and readability, sometimes with the restructuring of content. Also called substantive editing. See Chapters 4, 5, and 8 for more detail.

literary agent: see agent

manuscript evaluation: An assessment of the manuscript's readiness for publishing that identifies big-picture problems. See Chapters 5 and 7 for more detail.

metaphor: A figure of speech that compares two seemingly unrelated things to convey a fresh meaning, imbuing one thing with the qualities of another.

micro fiction: A type of very short fiction.

motivation: A character's reason for doing something. Can be conscious or unconscious, stated or implied.

narrative mode: On the page, fiction takes many forms, including scenes or scene fragments; exposition; narrative summary; excerpts from emails, diaries, or letters; interview transcripts; and authorial intrusions. These are "narrative modes." Most novels and stories use several narrative modes to achieve different effects on the page and influence the reading experience (e.g., snappy dialogue can speed up the reading experience, while complex interior monologue can slow it down).

narrative summary: Moves the story in time and/or place without going into details. Example:

> He spent one whole winter without lighting his stove, and
> used to declare that he liked it better, because one slept more
> soundly in the cold. For the present he, too, had been
> obliged to give up the university, but it was only for a time,
> and he was working with all his might to save enough to

return to his studies again. Raskolnikov had not been to see
him for the last four months, and Razumihin did not even
know his address.

Fyodor Dostoevsky, *Crime and Punishment*

narrator: The entity who tells a story.

novel: A fictional prose narrative, usually long and complex, relating some variety of human experience in the form of a story, often (at least in realistic fiction) with causally linked events.

novella: A fictional prose narrative, shorter than a novel but longer than a short story, usually relating a specific central experience. See Chapter 10 for more detail.

omniscient: Literally, all-seeing. A point of view in which any character's thoughts, feelings, and observations can be shown to the reader.

orphan: The first line of a paragraph appearing at the bottom of a page.

pacing: How quickly or slowly the story moves the reader through its events.

pass: A round of editing. See Chapter 4 for more detail.

plot: How the story is told—what happens, in what order, from whose point of view.

point of view (POV): The perspective through which events in a fictional narrative are experienced.

premise: What the story is about, in a nutshell, often described in terms of character, problem, stakes. Or as Lajos Egri puts it in *The Art of Dramatic Writing*, "a thumbnail synopsis." Egri suggests that the premise of *Romeo and Juliet* is "great love defies even death."

print-on-demand (POD): Printing book copies only after they have been ordered via publishers or retailers.

production: Creating a print or digital book from the edited manuscript.

proofread: This post-editing task checks the final text for any remaining errors before the book proceeds to publication. See Chapters 5 and 9 for more detail.

prose: A literary medium distinguished from poetry; the language used in writing.

protagonist: The subject of a story, the principal character in a literary work.

psychic distance: How far the reader gets inside the character's head; can range from close to very distant. Relates to point of view.

query letter: A one-page letter that introduces the novel to a prospective agent or publisher and invites their interest. Tells the story in miniature. Writing a query letter can be a good way to discover whether your story works.

resolution: The point in a novel at which the chief dramatic complication is worked out.

review tab: In Microsoft Word, this is where you access Track Changes and marginal comments.

scene: Characters in action in a specific place and time. Scenes can have narrative summary, exposition, dialogue, interior monologue (thinking and feeling), description, etc. Example:

> I rang the bell and was shown up to the chamber which had formerly been in part my own.
>
> His manner was not effusive. It seldom was; but he was glad, I think, to see me. With hardly a word spoken, but with a kindly eye, he waved me to an armchair, threw across his case of cigars, and indicated a spirit case and a gasogene in the corner. Then he stood before the fire and looked me over in his singular introspective fashion.
>
> "Wedlock suits you," he remarked. "I think, Watson, that you have put on seven and a half pounds since I saw you."
>
> "Seven!" I answered.
>
> "Indeed, I should have thought a little more. Just a trifle more, I fancy, Watson. And in practice again, I observe. You did not tell me that you intended to go into harness."
>
> "Then, how do you know?"
>
> "I see it, I deduce it. How do I know that you have been getting yourself very wet lately, and that you have a most clumsy and careless servant girl?" [etc.]
>
> Arthur Conan Doyle, *A Scandal in Bohemia*

scene fragment: Characters inserted into narrative summary to capture snippets of essential conversation or close-up action.

scene goals: Short-term goals within individual scenes that can move the story, add conflict, and increase tension.

search engine optimization (SEO): A process that involves using keywords in your book's website or a retailer's search engine listing with the goal of getting it to show up at the top of the list of results when those keywords are entered into a search engine by potential customers.

season: A period of time during which publishers release a batch of new books for sale. Book publishers can have two or three seasons per year, the major ones being spring and fall.

self-publishing: Producing and selling your own book at your own expense rather than through a publisher.

setting: The time, place, or circumstances in which the action takes place.

short story: A complete work of fiction between 1,000 and 15,000 words, approximately.

simile: A figure of speech comparing two unlike things, linked by the word "like" or "as."

story: A fictional narrative.

story world: Not just the physical location or setting of a novel, but also the overall milieu in which characters operate—social, economic, political, natural, technological, and other aspects of the world inhabited by a novel's characters. Story world is best delivered naturally, "in scene" or via exposition woven into scene, rather than in a monolithic block of description or exposition.

stream of consciousness: When the character's internal experience is given in a flow of ideas and feelings without logical organization.

structure: How the story is designed; its organization of parts within the coherent whole. Many novels are structured chronologically and use cause-and-effect to pull the reader through events from beginning to end, while other structures can be more complex, looping the story's events through time and space. Structure in fiction is integral to the story—it's not something imposed, but something that develops as you shape the events into an experience for the reader.

style: A particular manner of expression with a distinctive quality. In other words, it's how you write and what it feels like to read your writing. In copyediting, style refers to conventions with respect to spelling, punctuation, capitalization, and typographic arrangement (e.g., "Chicago style" means that the copyeditor is following the conventions laid out in *The Chicago Manual of Style*).

submit: To offer a manuscript to an acquisitions editor for possible publication.

substantive edit: A level of editing that works on prose at the sentence and paragraph level. Improves flow and readability, sometimes with restructuring of content. Also called line editing. See Chapters 4, 5, and 8 for more detail.

sudden fiction: A type of very short fiction.

symbol: A particular object or event that takes on thematic meaning.

tension: A state of suspense over what will happen next. Keeps the reader turning pages.

theme: Theme in a novel relates to a unifying or dominant idea that permeates the story. Looked at another way, it's what the story underneath the story is about. This subtle and cohering force permeates the work, borne out not just by the protagonist's experience, but by every character's.

three-act structure: Traditional three-act structure, in its simplest form, is composed of three 'acts': beginning, middle, and end. The beginning establishes the characters and story world and introduces the main problem or conflict and possibly subplots. The middle act, which is often the longest, develops the story, introduces further complications, shows the protagonist(s) struggling to get what they want or avoid what they don't want, and creates a sense of rising action toward a climax. The final act usually contains the climax, denouement and resolution. Three-act structure is just one of many possible structures, but the sense of a beginning, middle and end is so time-honored and instinctive in the human psyche that it can be useful to think in those terms when examining your novel's events.

throughline: The spine of the character's story as they move through events. Originally an acting term coined by Russian actor, director, and producer Constantin Stanislavsky (1863–1938). Characters should evolve, and thinking about their throughline is a way of seeing whether yours do. The throughline is formed by a character's goals, actions and evolution from scene to scene.

Track Changes: A feature of Microsoft Word that allows visible markup of an electronic manuscript by showing deletions, additions, and formatting changes.

trade publishing: Publishing general consumer titles for a mainstream audience, as distinguished from academic and other types of publishing.

tragedy: The story of a character's fall, often through personality flaws or through forces beyond the character's control.

turning point: The moment when a character or situation irrevocably shifts or changes direction in a substantial way.

university press: A publishing house connected to a university or college. Some university presses publish trade fiction as well as academic work.

voice: The writer's style in any given work. The same writer can produce novels with markedly different voices.

widow: The last line of a paragraph appearing at the top of a page.

writing coach: A type of editor / teacher who provides one-on-one support to a writer, often involving critiquing an ongoing project, providing information or resources, setting writing exercises, and meeting online or in person. See Chapter 7 for more detail.

Sources and Resources

Books and Essays

Appelbaum, Judith. *How to Get Happily Published: A Complete and Candid Guide.* 5th ed. New York: HarperCollins Publishers, Inc., 1998.

Arana, Marie, ed. *The Writing Life: Writers on How They Think and Work—A Collection from* The Washington Post *Book World.* New York: Public Affairs, 2003.

Bell, Susan. *The Artful Edit: On the Practice of Editing Yourself.* New York: W.W. Norton, 2007.

Booth, Wayne C. The Rhetoric of Fiction, 2nd ed. Chicago: University of Chicago Press, 1983.

Bronte, Charlotte. *Jane Eyre.* New York: The Modern Library Paperback Edition, 2000.

Brooks, Larry. *Story Fix: Transform Your Novel from Broken to Brilliant.* Cincinnati: Writer's Digest Books, 2015.

Burroway, Janet. *Writing Fiction: A Guide to Narrative Craft.* 5th ed. New York: Longman, 2000.

Butcher, J., Drake, C., & Leach, M. *Butcher's Copy-editing: The Cambridge Handbook for Editors, Copy-editors and Proofreaders.* Cambridge: Cambridge University Press, 2006.

Cavin, Ruth. "Editing Crime Fiction." In *Editors on Editing: What Writers Need to Know About What Editors Do*, edited by Gerald Gross, 194–202. New York: Grove Atlantic, 1993.

Cleaver, Jerry. *Immediate Fiction: A Complete Writing Course.* New York: St. Martin's Griffin, 2002.

Conan Doyle, Arthur. "A Scandal in Bohemia." In *The Adventures of Sherlock Holmes*. London: A&W Visual Library, 1975.

Cron, Lisa. *Wired for Story: The Writer's Guide to Using Brain Science to Hook Readers from the Very First Sentence.* New York: Ten Speed Press, 2012.

Cypher, Sarah. *The Editor's Lexicon: Essential Writing Terms for Novelists.* Portland: Glyd-Evans Press, 2010.

Dickens, Charles, ed. "All the Year Round." London: Chapman and Hall, 1859–1895.

Dillard, Annie. *The Writing Life.* New York: Harper Perennial, 1989.

Dostoevsky, Fyodor. *Crime and Punishment.* New York: Vintage Books, 1950.

Eco, Umberto. *Six Walks in the Fictional Woods.* Cambridge: Harvard University Press, 1994.

Egri, Lajos. *The Art of Dramatic Writing: Its Basis in the Creative Interpretation of Human Motives.* New York: Simon & Schuster, 1946.

Einsohn, Amy. *The Copyeditor's Handbook: A Guide for Book Publishing and Corporate Communications.* Berkeley: University of California Press, 2011.

Esquire. "The Napkin Project." February 2007: 96–101.

Field, Syd. *Screenplay: The Foundations of Screenwriting, A Step-by-Step Guide from Concept to Finished Script.* New York: Dell, 1982.

Freytag, Gustav. *Technique of the Drama: An Exposition of Dramatic Composition and Art, 3rd ed.* Chicago: Scott, Foresman and Company, 1900.

Gardner, John. *The Art of Fiction: Notes on Craft for Young Writers.* New York: Vintage Books, 1991.

George, Elizabeth. *Write Away: One Novelist's Approach to Fiction and the Writing Life.* New York: Perennial Currents, 2005.

Ginna, Peter, ed. *What Editors Do: The Art, Craft, and Business of Book Editing.* Chicago: University of Chicago Press, 2017.

Government Publishing Office. *Style manual: an official guide to the form and style of federal government publications.* Washington: US Government Publishing Office, 2016.

Gross, Gerald, ed. *Editors on Editing: What Writers Need to Know about What Editors Do. 3rd ed.* New York: Grove Press, 1993.

Hodgins, Jack. *A Passion for Narrative: A Guide for Writing Fiction.* Toronto: McClelland & Stewart, 1993.

Hugo, Richard. *The Triggering Town: Lectures and Essays on Poetry and Writing.* New York: W.W. Norton & Company, 1979.

James, Steven. *Story Trumps Structure: How to Write Unforgettable Fiction by Breaking the Rules.* Cincinnati: Writer's Digest Books, 2014.

Kawabata, Yasunari. *Palm-of-the-Hand Stories.* New York: Farrar, Straus and Giroux, 2006.

Korda, Michael. "Headbirths: Bookish Midwifery." In *The Writing Life: Writers on How They Think and Work—A Collection from The Washington Post Book World*, edited by Marie Arana, 187–193. New York: Public Affairs, 2003.

Lerner, Betsy. "What's Love Got to Do With It: The Author-Editor Relationship." In *What Editors Do: The Art, Craft & Business of Book Editing*, edited by Peter Ginna, 69–76. Chicago: University of Chicago Press, 2017.

Lerner, Betsy. *The Forest for the Trees: An Editor's Advice to Writers.* rev. ed. New York: Riverhead Books, 2010.

Lukeman, Noah. *The First Five Pages: A Writer's Guide to Staying Out of the Rejection Pile.* New York: Fireside, 2000.

McCarthy, Paul D. "Developmental Editing." In *Editors on Editing: What Writers Need to Know About What Editors Do*, edited by Gerald Gross, 134–142. New York: Grove Atlantic, 1993.

McCormack, Thomas. *The Fiction Editor, the Novel, and the Novelist: A Book for Writers, Teachers, Publishers, and Anyone Else Devoted to Fiction,* 2nd ed. Philadelphia: Paul Dry Books, 2006.

McKee, Robert. *Story: Substance, Structure, Style, and the Principles of Screenwriting.* York, UK: Methuen, 1999.

Norton, Scott. *Developmental Editing: A Handbook for Freelancers, Authors, and Publishers.* Chicago: University of Chicago Press, 2009.

Page, Shannon, ed. *The Usual Path to Publication: 27 Stories about 27 Ways In.* Cedar Crest: Book View Café Publishing Cooperative, 2016.

Percy, Benjamin. *Thrill Me: Essays on Fiction.* Minneapolis: Graywolf Press, 2016.

Pickett, Katherine. *Perfect Bound: How to Navigate the Book Publishing Process Like a Pro.* Silver Spring: Hop On Publishing, 2014.

Poynter, Dan. *The Self-Publishing Manual: How to Write, Print and Sell Your Own Book.* Santa Barbara: Para Publishing, 2007.

Prose, Francine. *Reading Like a Writer: A Guide for People Who Love Books and for Those Who Want to Write Them.* New York: Harper Perennial, 2006.

Russo, Richard. "In Defense of Omniscience." In *Bringing the Devil to His Knees: The Craft of Fiction and the Writing Life*, edited by Charles Baxter and Peter Turchi, 7–17. Ann Arbor: University of Michigan Press, 2001.

Saller, Carol Fisher. *The Subversive Copy Editor: Advice from Chicago (or, How to Negotiate Good Relationships with Your Writers, Your Colleagues, and Yourself).* 2nd ed. Chicago: University of Chicago Press, 2016.

Scheer, Laurie. *The Writer's Advantage: A Toolkit for Mastering Your Genre.* Studio City, CA: Michael Wiese Productions, 2014.

Snyder, Blake. *Save the Cat! The Last Book on Screenwriting That You'll Ever Need.* Studio City: Michael Wiese Productions, 2005.

Stanislavski, Constantin. *Building a Character.* New York: Routledge / Theatre Arts Books, 1994.

Stein, Sol. *How to Grow a Novel: The Most Common Mistakes Writers Make and How to Overcome Them.* New York: St. Martin's Griffin, 1999.

Strunk, William, Jr., and E. B. White. *The Elements of Style.* 2nd ed. New York: MacMillan Publishing Co., Inc., 1972.

The Best American Short Stories. New York: Houghton Mifflin Harcourt, 1915–present.

The Chicago Manual of Style: The Essential Guide for Writers, Editors, and Publishers, 17th ed. Chicago: University of Chicago Press, 2017.

The O. Henry Prize Stories: The Best Short Stories of the Year. New York: Anchor Books, 1919–present.

The Pushcart Prize: Best of the Small Presses. Wainscott: Pushcart Press, 1976–present.

The Year's Best Science Fiction & Fantasy. Germantown: Prime Books, 2010–present.

Wade, James O'Shea. "Doing Good–and Doing It Right." In *Editors on Editing: What Writers Need to Know About What Editors Do*, edited by Gerald Gross, 73–82. New York: Grove Press, 1993.

Warland, Betsy. *Breathing the Page: Reading the Act of Writing.* Toronto: Cormorant Books, 2010.

Whitney, Phyllis A. *Guide to Fiction Writing.* Boston: The Writer, Inc. Publishers, 1982.

Witte, George. "This Needs Just a Little Work: On Line Editing." In *What Editors Do: The Art, Craft & Business of Book Editing*, edited by Peter Ginna, 96–105. Chicago: University of Chicago Press, 2017.

Wood, James. *How Fiction Works.* New York: Picador, 2008.

Websites*

*This is an idiosyncratic list of the websites I like and use.

Editing

Editorial Freelancers Association	www.the-efa.org
EFA Rate Table	www.the-efa.org/rates/
Society for Editors and Proofreaders	www.sfep.org.uk
Editors Canada	www.editors.ca

Publishing

Book Industry Study Group	www.bisg.org
Jane Friedman's website	www.janefriedman.com
Publisher's Weekly	www.publishersweekly.com
Publisher's Marketplace	www.publishersmarketplace.com
Copyright & Fair Use (Stanford U)	www.fairuse.stanford.edu/
Literary Marketplace	www.literarymarketplace.com

Writing Magazines

Poets & Writers	www.pw.org
The Writer's Chronicle	www.awpwriter.org

Online Critique Groups

Critique Circle	www.critiquecircle.com
Scribophile	www.scribophile.com

Editorial Tools and Information

Book Mapping course	helloheidifiedler.com/workshops
Editorial Arts Academy	www.editorialartsacademy.com
A Writer's Roadmap	www.awritersroadmap.com

Permissions

Acknowledgments

This book exists because of all the writers I've worked with, who have not only given me deep experience in editing fiction but also taught me what it takes to be a writer today. Particular thanks to those who told me their stories about finding and working with fiction editors.

I first learned about the profound and lasting impact of good editorial feedback from Benjamin Percy, Claire Davis, and Craig Lesley in the MFA program at Pacific University. Thank you for giving me the wherewithal to do this work.

I'm grateful to my brother Chris Dobie for early help and to the writing friends who have critiqued drafts of the manuscript: Amanda Goldrick-Jones, Sharon Harrigan, Doug Harrison, Donna Shanley, Maureen Phillips, and Joanne Watson.

For her practical help and professional skills, many thanks to copyeditor Megan Lewis, who went above and beyond meticulous copyediting by gently pointing out errors and gaps in the text. Thanks also to AJ Boothe for her eagle eye. Any remaining errors are mine.

Much gratitude to designer Erek Tymchak for his inspiring cover, his design skills, and his kindness.

Most of all, I'm grateful to Richard, AJ, and Laurel Boothe, who've supported and encouraged my writing and editing vocations with understanding and love.

145

Index

About the Author

P.S. (PAT) DOBIE wrote her first novella in three days with no prior writing experience. To her great surprise it was published to positive reviews with almost no revision. Despite this, or maybe because of it, she became obsessed with the crafts of writing and editing, eventually founding Lucid Edit, where she helps other writers get their work ready to send out into the world.

Learn more about her at www.patdobie.com.

Thank you for reading!

- Wondering what a **book map** looks like? They've been called "witchcraft," but they're just a form of geekery that editors use for diagnosing problems with plot, pacing, and structure.
- Never used the invaluable tool called a **style sheet**? That's how editors keep track of important facts to ensure that your novel or series is correct and consistent.
- Curious about **editorial comments** and **manuscript markups**? See them for yourself by visiting the link below.

Visit www.awritersroadmap.com
to download a PDF showing these tools in action.

Made in United States
North Haven, CT
30 August 2022